A Child's Geography

Explore His Earth

Ann Voskamp

"Go into all the world..."
~ Mark 16:15

A Child's Geography is an endeavor of which a portion of profits support
World Vision, *an internationally recognized Christian relief,*
development and advocacy organization dedicated to
working with children, families and communities
to overcome poverty and injustice.

"Circle... take her measure... gaze long... climb ...
Then you can tell the next generation, detail by detail, the story of God." *~Ps. 48 12*

BRAMLEY BOOKS
www.bramleybooks.com
A Division of Knowledge Quest, Inc.

Published in the United States of America by:
Bramley Books
A Division of Knowledge Quest, Inc.
P.O. Box 789
Boring, OR 97009

www.achildsgeography.com
Copyright 2005 by Ann Voskamp
First Edition, Published 2005
Second Edition, Published 2007
Third Edition, Revised and Published 2008 by Knowledge Quest, Inc.
All rights reserved.
ISBN # 1-932786-32-5 / 978-1-932786-32-3

Cover design by Jeremy Conn of Conn Creative Media – www.conncreativemedia.com
Template designs for CD-ROM by Tonia Peckover
The Appendix was graciously and competently compiled by Ruth Marshall of
http://wonder.riverwillow.com.au/

Publisher's Cataloging-in-Publication data

Voskamp, Ann Marie.
    A child's geography : explore His earth / Ann Voskamp.
    p. cm.
    ISBN 1-932786-32-5
    Series : A Child's Geography, Vol. 1
    Summary : Readers get to know what's under our feet, over our heads and in the world around
      us: the atmosphere, the hydrosphere, the lithosphere, and then how to get around this world:
      maps, latitude and longitude.

1. Geography--Juvenile literature. 2. Geography. 3. Geography--Religious aspects--Christianity. I.
Title. II. Series.

G133 V67 2008
910.20--dc22   2008921557

A few travel thoughts before embarking

There is nothing nicer than curling up with a good book....and your children.
You are invited.
Come. Snuggle. Explore. Discover. Delight.
Worship our Creator.

READINGS

May I invite you to call the children, grab a blanket, and together begin the journey? If possible, read each chapter's main adventure text at one sitting. Then wrap up your read-aloud time with the notebooking segment, the writing of your postcard home.

Then, at the next sitting, you may choose to take up the segments *"Reaching out To His World"* and try one (or both!) of the *"Too-Fun-To-Resist Excursions."* **Dividing** the chapter into two sittings will keep your young geographer fresh and will encourage them to revisit the adventure in their minds when they return for the second sitting. (If you really don't think you will return for the second sitting, please be sure to then conclude your one reading with *"Reaching out to His World."* This segment is of the utmost importance. (See below for more information.)

SCHEDULING

Dividing your travels through *A Child's Geography* into two readings like this allows for various scheduling options. You may want to take up your geographical excursions twice per week, reading the chapter and notebooking on one day. Then, later in the week, returning to that adventure's *"Reaching Out to His World"* segment and the activity excursions. Or you may choose to embark on your geographical adventure only once per week, thus reading the chapter and notebooking one week and returning for the activities and *"Reaching Out to His World"* the following week.

NARRATIONS

Throughout the text are narration prompts: **Tell the folks at home all about it!** You may want to role-play a phone call with your young geographer for these narration prompts, you holding the phone, asking the narration questions, and your young geographer responding on his/her phone. Encourage your geographers to narrate whatever they recall. If, however, he/she seems at a loss, choose one or two of the **Memory Joggers** to kindle a more glowing narration. But give a child time to generate their own re-telling. **Memory Joggers** may also be used to highlight key discoveries of the adventure. Again, the narration prompts are merely guides to encourage a narration. It is best for learning and long-term memory to wait patiently and allow your young geographer to reconstruct the narration on his or her own. The **Memory Joggers** are guideposts to help map the way.

NOTEBOOKING

Travelers will be writing of their adventures on oversized, large pieces of cardstock. Postcard templates are available for you on the CD-ROM. It probably would be most convenient if you cut out a stack of a dozen oversized cards now — large enough so the geographer can write/notebook lots, small enough so as not to overwhelm the traveler with all that space to fill. You know your geographer best—cut the cardstock accordingly.

Ask any world traveler — if they don't log their journeys in a journal, so many details of the trip slip away, forever lost in a sea of long-forgotten memories. *Don't let that happen.* It only takes a moment to hand your geographer a pencil and piece of cardstock and get the adventure written down. (Or you may have your geographer orally narrate the postcard to you as you jot it down for them.) Even one or two lines of writing are better than neglecting the postcard entirely. Notebooking on a postcard after each adventure will deeply enrich your geographer's experience. *You can do this!*

REACHING OUT

Knowledge without love is an empty, heartbreaking gong. It would be a very sad state if our young geographers knew much of His world…but had hearts that were indifferent to the people with whom we share our home. What are we without love? As a teacher or parent nurturing the learning of children, it may be tempting to read the main text of each chapter and then omit the "***Reaching Out***" segment. May I gently exhort you to not only read through this segment in each chapter, but to follow through on its encouragements. We are called to be Christ's hands and heart to a hurting world. Let's not fail Him!

READING LISTS

Reading lists have been included at the end of every chapter. These titles are only suggested to supplement **A Child's Geography**. **None are necessary**. Your library may be a wonderful resource for more titles. Books from a creationist standpoint have been noted as such on the reading list. I encourage you to peruse all books before sharing with your young geographer. Some titles may have had wonderful graphics that are most beneficial, while the text may not uphold God as Creator. Weigh the balance, and, knowing your own geographers and family situation, trust your own discernment.

ACTIVITIES

The optional activities are just that—**optional**. The text of each chapter is the substance, or the "meat", of the learning. The activities are simply supplemental, or "dessert." Please do not feel obligated to do the activities. Each of the "***Too-Fun-To-Resist Excursions***" were chosen because, Lord willing, they extended the learning of that chapter's adventure, they were simple and practically doable for a teacher with many responsibilities — and they were fun! Your young geographers may well be able to set out on many of the excursions by themselves. And if you can resist the excursions, you still will have enjoyed a grand adventure nonetheless!

COPYWORK

Geography Copywork for each chapter is included on the CD-ROM. Encourage your geographers to copy out the definitions, Scripture, appropriate hymns and poetrythat correspond with the chapter reading. Not only will doing so solidify knowledge discovered, expand your geographer's horizons, and give further written record to the journey, the act of transcribing has far-reaching language arts benefits. Determine which combination of notebooking and copywork will work best for your family. Again, do not feel obligated to do it all. The copywork selections may also be used for **Recollections**---reviewing and recalling previous adventures!

RECOLLECTIONS

Often review your postcards on a ring to recall past travels—perhaps before adding a new postcard, briefly review past explorations. Feel free to briefly review the definitions of past travels (from the copywork section on the CD-ROM) before heading out on your next adventure. Consistent trips down memory lane of past chapters will keep the adventures and knowledge fresh---and soon those discoveries will be a natural part of your geographers' tales!

BOARDING PASSES READY?

With the traveling details now nicely attended to, I invite you to step on board to memorable adventures across His glorious globe! Hold on to your hats, folks — His world will take your breath away! And don't forget to drop a postcard in the mail, telling the folks at home all about it!

"The whole earth is full of
His glory!"
~Isaiah 6:3

Adventure Notes

AUNTIE EM,
THERE IS NO PLACE LIKE HOME

Chapter 1

Have you ever pulled an old blanket over a table, dragged in some pillows and stuffed friends and stood back to admire your new home? Or hammered together some planks of wood high up in a tree, then climbed up amongst the leafy branches and called it **"Home"**?

Home is where we all belong, a place we come back to, a place just for us.

Perhaps you call home a secluded cabin tucked away in quiet woods? An apartment overlooking the twinkling lights of the city? A hut squatting on stilts in a tangle of jungle clearing? A floating boat, docked at the end of a pier?

Every person, everywhere, has a home.

Once when my little brother was at the zoo, he got lost, and couldn't find his way home. And a kind man stopped to ask the teary-eyed little fellow where his home was. What did it look like? How big was it? Did he know the name of the people who lived in his home?

Do you think he responded something like this?

"My home is held up in the middle of space. Home is like a big, round ball, slowly turning so every twelve hours it soaks in warm sunshine and then sleeps the next 12 hours in darkness. My home is so big more than 6 billion people, speaking several thousand languages, live there — along with lions and parrots and beluga whales and polar bears and pythons. And there are 350 million cubic miles of water to sail about right in my home!"

If my brother had explained his home like that, wouldn't the man have been most surprised? He would have wanted to know WHO could make a home like THAT!

My brother would have said, "God made a home like that! He made it not with wood and nails, or bricks and mortar, but simply by speaking the earth into being. He spoke the words, "*Let there be light. Let there be a firmament in the midst of the waters, and let it divide the waters from the waters*" (Gen. 1) and there was my home—EARTH!"

Earth is home to all people everywhere. And God made our home like no other home that has ever been made! Would you like a brief tour of our home?

If you do, that makes you a **geographer**! What is a geographer? Someone like you—someone who wants to explore our home, Earth, to ask questions about what is under our feet and over our heads, to ask why some areas of our home look so very different from other areas, and to meet all the different kinds of people who live in your home with you!

Geographers study geography. The word "**geography**" comes from the

This is a copy of the very first picture ever taken of the whole of our Earthly home. Photographed some 30,000 km. (18,641 miles) out in space, south is at the top while North America is in the bottom right. **NASA**

Greek language and simply means "*to write about the earth.*" So, together, let's be geographers and write about God's home for us, Earth!

While your home has a front door, and maybe a back door, perhaps an upstairs or a downstairs, the home God made for us has no front or back, top or bottom. That is because our earth is like a big ball. Geographers (like you and me) refer to earth as a "*sphere*" because in Latin "**sphere**" means "*ball.*"

While I could see your home from the street, you can't see the home God made for us by standing back a little. The home God made for us is much bigger than just what you see outside your window, bigger than what is down your street, bigger even than what is across your country. The home God made for us is STUPENDOUSLY HUGE!! So huge, we can't really see it all! That sounds strange, doesn't it?

Have you ever laid your forehead against someone else's forehead and looked into their eyes? What did they look like? They looked like ALL eyes, didn't they? You were so close to their eyes, you didn't even see their toes, did you? But what if you ran to the very far end of the street and looked back at the same person? Wouldn't that same person who was once ALL eyes, now seem very small? You wouldn't be able to see their eyes, or even their toes, now. But now you could see the whole shape of the person.

When you look out your window, and see our earth, that is much like looking eye to eye with another person. You are so close to earth, you can't see all the parts of our home. If you wanted to see more of our earth you would have to go further than the end of your street, further away from earth even than an airplane. You would have to go way, way, WAY back into outer space to see our home, Earth, it is so big.

Just how big is Earth? Are you ready for some VERY astounding numbers?

Let's say there was one flat path all around the world. Then say you stuck a flag in the dirt and began walking down that long path around our home of Earth. If you walked ten long hours every day, you might cover slightly more than 22 miles (35 km.) every day. If you did that every single day, rain or shine, until you walked back to your flag, you would have walked the 24,860 miles (39,990 km.) all the way around Earth! Not only is that one very long walk, but you would be almost 3 years older—and have worn out a LOT of shoes!!!

The surface area, how much area our earth takes up, is 196,951,000 square miles (316,894,000 km.)! That means you would have to have 733 states of Texas to fill up this home God made for us!

Do you know how heavy our home is? The mass of Earth is a whopping 6.6 billion trillion tons (6 trillion trillion kilograms)! That is how much 1,100 million, million, million elephants would weigh!! Imagine the bathroom scale reading that ENORMOUS number!

God has made us a very impressive home, don't you think? To think that it was made simply by God's command! The Bible says that our world was not created through natural processes but directly by God Himself: **"...[T]he worlds were prepared by the word of God, so that what is seen was not made out of things which are visible"** (Heb. 11:3). That means that everything you see around you came into being from things that *can't* be seen! Everything you see came into being by God's *words*! And *that* was how our home called Earth was made!

Tell the folks at home all about it!

*What a home we live in! Tell us everything you know about your home of earth! (**Memory Joggers**: What is the shape of our home? How many people live in this home? What do we call people who write about Earth? Why is Earth referred to as a "sphere"? Tell me about how big and massive our Earth is. How did our home of Earth come into being?) There truly is no place like our home!*

I have never gone so far back, all the way to outer space in a rocket, and looked back at our home! Neither have you! (But maybe someday you will have such an incredible experience to gaze upon the beauty of Earth from up in a space ship! For now, we must be satisfied with pictures.)

A home for us all, **created by the WORD of His mouth!**

NASA

But there are men and women, called astronauts, who have flown some 370 miles (595 km.) way up into the universe on a space craft. Pressing their faces against the windows of the space shuttle, they have peered down at our home, Earth. How do you picture what our home looks like? Can you describe it?

An American Astronaut named Edgar Mitchell described Earth from space as "**a sparkling blue and white jewel, a light, delicate sky-blue sphere laced with slowly swirling veils of white, rising gradually like a small pearl in a thick sea of black mystery. It takes more than a moment to fully realize this is Earth .... Home**."

Isn't it strange that Astronaut Mitchell had lived his whole life in his home but when he saw it from space, he didn't quite recognize it at first?! He had probably never thought of his home looking like a shimmering jewel in an ocean of blackness! Did you think our home looked like that?

A Saudi Arabian Prince and astronaut, Sultan Bin Salmon Al-Saud, said this when looking down at our world from space, "**The first day or so, we (astronauts) all pointed to our (different) countries. The third or fourth day, we were pointing to our continents. By the fifth day, we were aware of only one Earth**." Think of it---only one Earth, one home for all of us.

Another American Astronaut described Earth like *"a **Christmas tree ornament hanging in the blackness of space. As we got farther and farther away it diminished in size. Finally it shrank to the size of a marble, the most beautiful marble you can imagine. That beautiful, warm, living object looked so fragile. Seeing Earth from space makes a man appreciate the creation of God and the love of God**."*

Aren't you thankful someone made the house you live in? A place for you to play and read and come in for dinner, a place with clean clothes and a warm bed—a place for you. How much more thankful we are that God made our Earth home! A place for us to breathe and run, discover and delight in—a place for all of us.

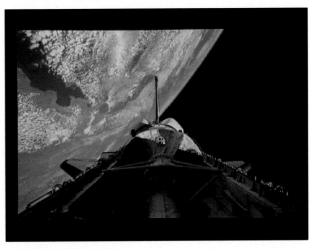

Flying 595 km (370 miles) overhead in space, do you recognize your home?   *NASA*

POSTCARD HOME

When you move into a new place to live, don't you want to tell everyone all about it? Why not share the wonder of Earth with someone! Cut a piece of cardstock to the dimensions of an oversized postcard. Draw and color what our home looks like from space. Then on the back of your postcard, write about our home of Earth. What does is look like from space? How large is our world? What are some magnificent facts about our home of Earth? Write it all down on your postcard. Then punch a hole in the upper right hand corner of your postcard and place your large post card on your ring. You've just completed your first postcard in your geographic adventures! But this is JUST the beginning!

(Postcard templates are available on the CD-ROM in the back of your book)

Reaching Out
to His World

Where do you sleep every night? Perhaps you have your own room, or share a room with a sibling. Maybe you even snuggle into the very same bed with a brother or sister. But you have a pillow somewhere that is just yours!

God made a home for *each* of us: Earth! There are folks, however, who live in our grand home of Earth...but don't have a place with a pillow just for them. We call these people **homeless.** Yes, homeless people *do* have a home: Earth. Homeless folks, however, do not have a roof over their heads, a safe place to eat dinner every night, or a place of their own to lay down with a pillow each night. Some of those who have no place in the world to call home are children younger than you! It is estimated that more than 100 *million children* on our Earth are homeless. Can you imagine a football stadium full of 55,000 *children*? Well, try to picture in your mind, *1,818 stadiums*, each full of a sea of only children, without adults. That gives you a picture in your mind of the vast number of children who have no place to come home to—tonight.

So where do homeless children spend their days and nights if they have no home with a roof or windows? Homeless children live on the streets of cities. They beg for their food or root through the garbage, looking for something edible. While some wrap themselves up in newspapers and sleep in back alleys, others are too often scared to sleep on the streets at night. Would you want to sleep out on the sidewalk in the dark? That is why many street children, throughout the world, fall asleep in big underground pipes underneath cities.

One boy named Joby who has slept for the last 9 years in the windowless, smelly pipes with many other children said, "*Everyone here would like to have their own family and* **home**."

Yes, everyone would like their very own home, with a door and a window and someone to love them. God said, "**It is not good that the man should be alone**" (Gen. 2:18). So God created us to take care of each other in our home we call Earth.

What could you do to reach out to people, adults and children, who have no place to come home to tonight?

- **Pray** together right now for the homeless and the street children—that they would feel the love of God in a very real way today.

- Do you know of a homeless person in your community? Maybe you could make a lunch and take it to them, invite them to your place for a meal, or just simply smile and talk with them today. Showing the love of God makes our Earth a better home for us all.

- We all want a home to come home to. And there are groups of individuals who build homes for the homeless. Perhaps you could get involved! **Habitat for Humanity** is one such worldwide ministry. Over the last 30 years, volunteers just like you have given freely of their time to help Habitat for Humanity build more than 175,000 homes for more than 750,000 people all over our Earth. Perhaps you can look for a Habitat for Humanity group near you and help them build a home someone can come home to!

(You can find Habitat for Humanity on the web at: http://www.habitat.org/)

Further Explorations

Earth From Above for Young Readers *by Yann Arthus-Bertrand*

(Gr. 4 and higher) Photographer Arthus-Bertrand leans outs of a helicopter snapping bird-eyes views from all over the world. A breathtaking view of God's home for us, twenty-two scenes highlight African landscapes while the remaining photographs introduce other continents. (If you can't find this book, you simply cannot afford to miss the photographs at his website at http://www.yannarthusbertrand.com)

Children from Australia to Zimbabwe : a photographic journey around the world
by Maya Ajmera & Anna Rhesa Versola

This unique alphabet books introduces children from all over their world and the unique places they each call home.

If the world were a village: a book about the world's people *by David J. Smith*

(Gr. 3-5, younger for reading aloud) Author David Smith makes the notion of our world more accessible by imagining the world as village of only 100 people. How many computers are owned in the global village? What we take for granted is appreciated through new, grateful eyes. A very informative, memorable book, that will raise awareness of how our home of Earth is experienced by our other family members.

Endeavor views the earth *compiled by Robert A. Brown*

"'What you would have seen out the windows of the Space Shuttle had you traveled with us.' Jay Apt, astronaut."

Earth from space *by Andrew K. Johnston*

(Older children) Join Smithsonian geographer Johnston as he photographs earth from space. Stunning satellite images introduce readers to scenes from our home such as the Grand Canal in Venice and what Earth looks like at night.

The Home planet *by Kevin W. Kelley*

(Older children) Gaze on 150 photographs of Earth taken from space. Read the accompanying by quotes from astronauts. What does an ``Earthrise'' look like, as seen from *the* moon? View our mountain ranges, canyons, coastlines, tropical storms and volcanoes from thousands of miles over our planet's surface. Reflect on the space explorers' realization that we are all part of one family here on Earth and the Earth a precious gift not to be neglected.

A House is a House for Me *by Mary Ann Hoberman*

(Gr. 1-3) A delightful book of rhyme, this book is a classic you will revisit again and again. Soon you will be seeing houses and homes everywhere---and will want to write your own version of A House is a House for Me! A lyrical, amusing way to introduce the notion that we all have homes everywhere... and the earth is a home for us all!

Too-Fun-to-Resist Excursion!

AND THIS IS THE HOME THAT GOD BUILT!

Our earthly home is a pretty big place! It would be very easy to get lost. Do you know where in our home you are?!! Let's see if together we can draw it out so we *know* more about the home that God built for you!

Materials needed:

~ a large piece of paper
~ pencil and crayons or pencil crayons

~ globe or atlases

Ready To Go? Let's Head Out!

~ Draw a relatively small picture of you on your piece of paper.

~ Now draw your house around you. Then draw your street. See if you can now draw a circle where your town is around your home.

~ Next, sketch out the shape of your state or province around your city. Are you beginning to see how BIG our home of Earth really is?!!

~ Draw your country around your state. Then your continent around your country!

~ Now, the LAST part of your home to draw! Draw EARTH around it all!

Can you now to point to the various features of your drawing as you sing along:

> *"This is the Earth that*
> *holds the continent ,*
> *that holds the country,*
> *that holds the state,*
> *that holds the city,*
> *that holds the town,*
> *that holds the street,*
> *that holds the house,*
> *that is the home God built for me!"*

Take some time to write the actual names of your street, town, state, country, and continent on your drawing? Didn't God build an awe-inspiring home for us!?

Too-Fun-to-Resist Excursion!

MAKE YOUR OWN GLOBE!

We could never make a world as magnificent or amazing as the world God has made for us! You could, however, make your own small copy of our globe. God made our grand and glorious world in 7 days—and it may take you nearly that long just to make a replica globe that you can hold in your hands! And as you make your globe, think about how God made this entire planet of Earth by just *speaking* it into existence! Doesn't that make you want to praise Him?

Materials needed:

~ A round balloon
~ Lots of newspapers
~ Flour and water
~ An empty plastic container
~ Spoon

~ Pencil
~ Blue and Green paint
~ Paint Brushes
~ Marker

<u>Ready To Go? Let's Head Out!</u>

(Remember, God did not need to gather materials when He made Earth---He just *spoke* the Word, and things came into being! And *that* is truly awe-inspiring!)

~ First, get out a saucepan and mix 1 cup of flour into 1 cup of water until the mixture is thin. Stir into 4 cups of boiling water. Simmer for just a few minutes, then cool.

~ Then, tear a newspaper into lots and lots of strips. The strips should be about as wide as the length of your thumb (or about 1 inch). The strips can be any length.

~ Now take a deep breath and blow up your balloon. Tie it tight!

~ Roll up your sleeves and get ready for the gooey part! Dip each strip of paper into your water and flour glue, wipe off the excess with your fingers, and wrap the strip around the balloon. Cover the balloon with wet strips of paper. Cover the balloon in three coats of strips, but let your "globe" dry between the application of each layer for at least 8 hours (or overnight).

Once you have completed your three layers, let the globe dry completely. When your globe is completely dry, the balloon will usually pop by itself.

~ Now sharpen your pencil and pull out your atlases, or place an already finished globe in front of you. Mark a dot at the top and bottom of your globe with a pencil. One dot will represent the North Pole, the other dot will represent the South Pole.

Can you draw on your globe the area of land you live in? That shape of land is called a continent. What shape is that area of land, your continent? How big is it in relation to the globe? How far away is it from your dots of the North and South Pole? Looking at your atlas or finished globe, draw your continent on your globe.

Good for you! Now, asking yourself the same questions, draw the other continents on your globe. Don't forget any! (Drawing continents is challenging, isn't it? To think that God made REAL continents by just commanding it to be so!)

~ Now your globe needs some color! Lay out a bed of newspapers and paint each of your continents a dark green color to represent land. When you are finished, set your globe aside to dry.

~ God created water on the 2nd day of creation---so you need to now paint the rest of your small globe a brilliant sea blue! Again, lie out a bed of newspapers and paint around all of the green continents a watery blue to represent oceans and seas.

~ When the paint has dried, stand back and smile at your handmade globe! Can you take a marker and draw an x on the place where you live on Earth?

Finally write on your globe, "**O Lord, it is You who made the heavens and the Earth and the sea, and all that is in them.**" (Acts 4:24)

Yes, God made this marvelous Earth for us! And that should make us REALLY smile!

PEELING AN ONION

Chapter 2

When I was a child, I liked looking into folks' windows as we drove by in late evenings. What hung on the walls inside those houses? (We used to drive by one home that had a huge star quilt sprawled over one whole wall!) What colors glowed from within the homes? (One of the grand, formal houses in town had brilliant fire-engine red walls!)

But there were some houses I never got to see inside—their curtains were always drawn disappointingly shut. I could only imagine what surprises lay behind those heavy blinds.

Our earth home has its own curtains. Earth is shrouded in curtains of air. Before we can explore our home of Earth, we first need to examine these curtains! These curtains of air are part of Earth, just like the skin of an onion is part of the onion.

We have a big word for that curtain of air wrapping up the Earth. We call it our "**atmosphere.**" Even though it is a big word, we can break it down into its parts to figure it out. "**Atmos**" comes from the Greek language and means "*vapor.*" That is what our clouds and air are made of, water vapor. "**Sphere**" comes from the Latin language, meaning "*ball.*" So atmosphere is literally the vapor wrapped around our ball. Just like an onion needs its skin to protect it, God made our atmosphere to keep everything in our home alive!

What ingredients did God use when He made our atmosphere? Simply, God organized the most perfect combination imaginable when He created the atmosphere! The atmosphere surrounding our Earth is composed of gases. This is not the kind of gas you fill the fuel tank of your car with, but these gases are the precise gases God knew life on Earth needed to live. A **gas** is a substance with no fixed volume or shape but expands to fill any volume of space available. Our atmosphere is composed of 78% nitrogen, 21% oxygen and trace amounts of other gases.

When I was a baby, my mother swaddled me in a blanket. You, too, probably have baby pictures of you sweetly tucked in a blanket. God wrapped up Earth in these gases because they too act like a protective blanket around us. They keep the heat the Earth needs inside the atmosphere. These gases also guard the Earth from much of the sun's dangerous rays called ultraviolet radiation. Isn't it amazing how God made our atmosphere perfect for life on Earth?

But there is more! God provided exactly the right amount of each of these gases in our atmosphere. What do we need to breathe? That's right—oxygen. There is 21% oxygen in the atmosphere. Why didn't God include more? Wouldn't that have been a good idea? NO! Oxygen easily reacts with other gases. If there were even an increase of only 1 percent more of oxygen—to 22%—there would be a 70 percent increase in the likelihood of forest fires flaming across the planet! Wasn't God a Master Builder when He made our home Earth?

Can you see Earth's curtain of atmosphere from this space-side seat?   NASA

Have you ever taken the skin off an onion? In the midst of rubbing your eyes (for onions can really sting your eyes!), what did you notice? Did you notice that there were several layers of skins wrapped around your onion? The atmosphere that wraps itself around our Earth is made up of more than just one layer, just like that onion you peeled had more than one layer of skin. (But thankfully, our atmosphere does not cause our eyes to tear up!)

Tell the folks at home all about it!

Tell me about this atmosphere that wraps itself around Earth. (**Memory Joggers**: *What does the word "atmosphere" mean? What is our atmosphere made of? Why did God wrap Earth in these gases? What did God create in the atmosphere that we need to breathe to live? Why did He not create more oxygen?) Don't you marvel at the wisdom of our Creator?*

Like that very first layer of onion, the one closest to the center, or core, of the onion, let's take a peek at the first layer of atmosphere, the layer we actually walk around in every day here on Earth. The layer that first blankets Earth is called the "**troposphere.**" Do you have any ideas why the first layer of vapor around our earth is called troposphere? Let's again be detectives and figure out its meaning. "**Tropos**" stems from the Greek word meaning "*turning*" or "*mixing.*" Can you guess what is turning and mixing in the layer of air around our sphere?

Yes, you can look up and actually see those vapors turning and mixing—the clouds right above your head! It is in this layer of the atmosphere that all of our storms and rain clouds and lightning occur. The troposphere certainly has a lot of weather happening in it, for it extends from the floor of our home, the Earth's surface, to 5-9 miles (8-14 km.) high over our ball home!

If you could walk UPWARDS (which none of us can, of course, but let's pretend), it would take you several hours of steady walking to walk up through the troposphere! But before you head out as a tourist in the Earth's atmosphere, remember your coat, hat and mittens, because the further you walk through the troposphere, the colder the temperatures! That's because the surface of our earth warms up the air. As you walk away from earth, the air cools. For every mile up walked through the troposphere, the temperature falls by 18 degrees F! (6.5 degrees C per kilometer) At the coldest, it would be -63 degrees F (-52 C). That is much colder than the inside of your freezer! Better pull your hat down! And you would be walking up through billowing, swirling clouds and zooming jets—so watch your step up there!

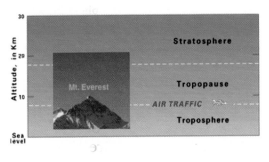

Mount Everest peaks halfway up into the troposphere—and has two thirds less oxygen than outside your front door!   *NASA*

As you keep walking through the troposphere layer of the atmosphere, you might be gasping for breath! That's because the higher you travel in the Earth's atmosphere, the less oxygen there is available for you to breathe. As you reached the 5-mile mark in the troposphere (halfway through the troposphere) you would have climbed as high as Mount Everest and there would be 2/3 less oxygen for you to breathe than when you hiked out your front door!

You also would be walking much slower. For every four steps you were treading when you started out on this journey, you now are only making one step! When you can't breathe very well, you can't walk very fast either! So, be sure when you grab your hat and mittens, to haul some tanks full of oxygen and an oxygen mask out the door with you as you begin your tour through the atmosphere!

Are you ready to peel another layer of the atmosphere off of Earth, just like peeling a layer of skin off an onion? If you were still feeling energetic and up to more walking, you would now walk into the next layer of our earth's atmosphere called the *"stratosphere."* What do you think stratosphere means? Remember that atmosphere means vapor around our ball, and troposphere means the turning (of vapor) around our ball. Stratosphere means a spreading out (*stratus* means *spreading out* in Latin) around our ball.

You would be getting pretty far away from your front door by now! The stratosphere is the second layer wrapped around earth and it extends 30 miles (50 km) above the ground of our home, Earth. But the further you kept on walking, you might even take *off* your hat and mittens! (It is not because you have worked yourself into a sweat, either!) The temperature would have risen from –63 F (-52C) in the troposphere to a balmy, much warmer 27F (-3C) up here in the stratosphere!

Hey, wait a minute! Wasn't it that the *further* away you got from earth, the *colder* the air became? So why are you getting *warmer* up here in the stratosphere, if you are further away from Earth?

The stratosphere has another layer spread out within it (remember *stratus* means spread out?) called an ozone layer. **Ozone** comes from the Greek word *"ozein"* which means *"to smell."* If you took a deep whiff up here in the ozone layer, you'd notice a very unusual odor. It is this layer of ozone that causes the temperature to become *warmer* in the stratosphere.

Tell the folks at home all about it!

What can you tell us about the troposphere and the stratosphere? (**Memory Joggers**: *What is the layer of atmosphere called that we live and walk around in everyday on Earth? What does "tropos" mean? What occurs in the troposphere? What happens to the temperature as you travel up through the troposphere? What does stratosphere mean? Do you remember how far from Earth the stratosphere extends? And what is the temperature like in the stratosphere? What does the word "ozone" mean?) Let's discover more now about ozone!*

Have you ever used a net to catch fish? You may have scooped up some little minnows and a tadpole or two. But still on the surface of the water may be some water striders or smaller minnows that your net didn't catch.

The ozone layer up in the stratosphere is much like a big net, catching some ultraviolet rays from the sun but still allowing some ultraviolet rays to reach earth. This layer of ozone, absorbing a great deal of the ultraviolet rays from the sun, dramatically heats up the stratosphere and *that* is why you are much warmer here than you were back in the troposphere!

Why do some ultraviolet rays from the sun need to be trapped in the intricate net of the ozone layer while other rays reach earth? Without the filtering effect of the ozone layer, the sun's *full* radiation would reach earth and harm plants, animals, and people. Have you ever had a nasty sunburn after a day of making sand castles at the beach? Then you have experienced the harmful, painful effect of the sun's radiation.

Some ultraviolet radiation, however, still does need to reach our Earth home. First, some of those rays are needed to reach our home to keep Earth's temperature warm enough for us—and plants and animals. Secondly, some of those ultraviolet rays from the sun are needed to encourage the working of vitamin D in our bodies. Vitamin D helps turn the calcium in our bodies into hard bones. Otherwise, our bones would break much easier! (If you have ever had your arm or leg in a cast, you certainly can appreciate the importance of strong bones—and the sun's rays!) God perfectly balanced how much ultraviolet radiation from the sun should reach earth when He designed the ozone layer up in the stratosphere!

Can you see the bad ozone hovering over our earthly home? *NASA*

You are the same kid, wherever you are. But if we caught you with your hand stuck in the cookie jar, we might say, "Bad!" And if we later found you embracing your crying baby brother, we might say "Good!" Whether we said bad or good would depend on where we found you! And the same is true of ozone!

What are these factories spewing?

National Parks Service

No matter where one finds ozone, its composition, what it is made of, remains the same. But, depending where ozone is *found*, ozone is either "bad ozone" or "good ozone." Ozone is "good ozone" if one finds it where God created ozone to be—in the stratosphere. Ozone is "good" here because high up in the stratosphere it protects us and all of Earth from harmful ultraviolet radiation from the sun. But ozone that is found lower, down here in the troposphere where we walk around, is "bad ozone." Just like God did not create you to be found with your hand stealing out of the cookie jar, God also did not create ozone to be found down here in the troposphere! Instead, it is *people* on Earth who have created the "bad ozone" of the troposphere. All of us on Earth create "bad ozone" when we drive cars and build large factories that spew fumes and exhaust out into our troposphere. Then the powerful ozone reaction that is meant to happen way up in the stratosphere against dangerous ultraviolet rays happens down here in the troposphere on *us*! That bad ozone reacts powerfully on you and me, making us sick to our stomach, causing us to cough or making it hard for us to breathe (which is an ailment called asthma). All of which God *never* intended for ozone to do. So think of ozone this way: Good up high, bad nearby.

Now that we have examined the good ozone of the stratosphere, let's take a look around the rest of the stratosphere. Since the warmer air lies *above* the nippier air in the stratosphere, the air doesn't turn around much in the stratosphere like it did back in the troposphere. Can you guess what you might see as a tourist of the stratosphere? You might notice debris floating around from volcanoes that exploded down on Earth years and years ago—when you were just a really little kid!

If we now stomp right out of the stratosphere, we will find ourselves in the **mesosphere.** It is time to pull down that knitted hat of yours and wrap yourself in a scarf because it is going to get REALLY COLD! The mesosphere, which begins just above the stratosphere and extends to 53 miles (85 km) high, has temperatures that again fall as low as –135 F (-93 C)! That is nearly TWICE as cold as the troposphere—and MUCH colder than your freezer!

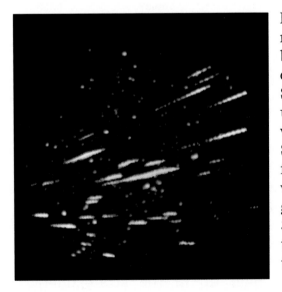

This photograph captures the Alpha-Monocerotid meteor outburst in 1995. Aren't you grateful that God created Earth with an atmosphere to protect us from these rock debris? *NASA*

Don't pull your scarf too high over your nose! Firstly, there is not enough oxygen to breathe up here in the mesosphere so you'll definitely be wearing your oxygen mask. Secondly, you don't want to miss anything up here in the mesosphere. Do you know what the mesosphere's main attraction is? Shooting stars! Meteors, pebble-size fragments floating around in space, glow with the heat of friction as they collide with gases in the mesosphere. Whizzing by at 30 miles (48 km) per second towards Earth, these "falling stars" usually burn up before they reach our Earth home way below. This is a good thing because no one wants to get hit by meteors that come flying Earth's way! God's atmosphere again protects us in marvelous ways. (But you don't have to gallivant through the mesosphere to catch a glimpse of these "meteor showers." At certain times of the year, especially in August and December, you can spot cascades of gleaming meteors right in your own backyard on earth—which would be a lot warmer than up here in the mesosphere!)

Well, congratulations! You've just walked through the troposphere, the stratosphere and the mesosphere, all of which is called "**Lower Atmosphere**"! Wasn't it an "out-of-this-world" adventure?! Quite the traveler, you are! Give yourself a pat on the back! And rest up for our next expedition when we head up through the Upper Atmosphere!

Tell the folks at home all about it!

Tell me more about where we have explored today. (**Memory Joggers**: Why did God create an ozone layer in the stratosphere? Why does some ultraviolet radiation need to reach Earth? What can you tell us about good ozone and bad ozone? What else might you discover floating in the stratosphere? What layer of the atmosphere lies above the stratosphere? What can you share about the mesosphere?)

POSTCARD HOME

Have you ever visited somewhere and sent a postcard home to a friend? What did you write in your letter home? World travelers often send home postcards telling of the grand sites they've seen and their adventures in new places!

Why don't you draw a picture of your atmosphere adventure on the front of a piece of postcard size piece of paper. Make sure you draw in all the layers you've toured in the atmosphere, so your friend knows where you've been! Then on the back of your postcard, why not write down some of the highlights from each layer in the Lower Atmosphere—what did you see or experience in the troposphere, the stratosphere and the mesosphere?

Punch a hole in the top corner of your card and place it on a ring. Soon you'll have more postcards to add on that ring of all of your travels! Oh, the places you'll go! (Postcard templates are available on the CD-ROM in the back of your book)

Reaching Out
to His World

Have you ever lived in a home that wasn't yours but you rented from the owner? Perhaps you live in an apartment or home where you pay monthly to the owner for the freedom to live there. Did you know that all of us live on our home of Earth and we don't own it? And we don't even have to pay rent!

God made our Earthly home in glorious and wise ways—and it is His! The Bible says: **"The earth is the Lord's and all it contains"** (Ps. 24:1). Those of us living on Earth need to remember that the Earth is not actually ours. It belongs to Him.

And we need to be wise caretakers and stewards of this home He has provided for us to live in. God has given us the privilege of living here "[T]**he earth He has given to the sons of men"** (Ps. 115:16). How we need to show Him our gratitude for the magnificent gift of Earth that He has given for our use!
So **what can you do to reach out** and take care of the Earth that belongs to God and He has allowed us to live in?

Ride a bike instead of driving!

We can make efforts *not* to make "bad ozone" —because bad ozone hurts people, crops and every thing alive in God's world. (Did you know that bad ozone can damage leaves so that the leaf dies or becomes spotted? Bad ozone kills the plants God has given us on Earth!)

Perhaps you can decide to do one of the following to take care of the Earth we live in:

~Burn calories and energy—not fuel. Walk whenever you can instead of driving. Every vehicle driving down all the roads all over our Earth emits gases that react with sunlight to create "bad ozone." So every time you decide not to drive somewhere, you make less bad ozone....and take good care of God's Earth.
~ Take the bus whenever you can or carpool with another family.
~Use water based paints since oil-based paints emit bad ozone-forming pollutants.

"As each one has received a special gift [like the privilege of living on this home, our Earth], **employ it in serving one another as good stewards**..." (I Pet. 4:10-11). So let's not make "bad ozone" nearby but preserve the "good ozone" up high!

Further Explorations

Atmosphere: sea of air *by Roy A. Gallant*

What causes violent storms, awe-inspiring rainbows, sunsets, and the sky's deep blue color? This book offers answers to such queries! With nearly conversational prose, Gallant's facts are thorough while the ideas are clearly explained for curious explorers.

The sky's the limit: all about the atmosphere *by Mark Rauzon*

Check out this volume for an introduction of the atmosphere. Learn the purpose of each layer of the atmosphere and the relation between air, the sky, and weather.

Earth's atmosphere *[videorecording] / a production of Schlessinger Media*

Review your knowledge of space with aspiring astronauts, Malcolm and Stanley. Curious explorers will discover more about the layers of our atmosphere. Why is each layer important to the survival of life on our planet? How is the atmosphere responsible for weather? What is a barometer and how would you build one? This episode explores the answers to these questions!

How did we find out about the atmosphere? *by Isaac Asimov*

(Gr. 5-9)   Older students will find Asimov's explanation of the atmosphere most beneficial. After surveying early experiments which proved air's existence, Asimov turns to describing experiments which proved the existence of atoms, the density of air and the discovery of oxygen, nitrogen, hydrogen and gases. The volume concludes with an explanation the atmospheres of seven of the planets in our solar system.

The Sky Jumps into your Shoes at Night *by Jasper Tomkins*

(Gr. 1-3) What is the sky? Where is air? A whimsical perspective on the adventures of the sky, this fun text and watercolour illustrations foster an appreciation for our atmosphere and earth.

Too-Fun-to-Resist Excursion!

OZONE ALERT!

Recall how God created the stratosphere to include a layer of "good ozone" that protects all of us on Earth from dangerous ultraviolet radiation from the sun. But we on Earth create "bad ozone" here in the troposphere when we engage in activities such as driving cars and puffing fumes out of factories. Can you see this "bad ozone"? You may not be able to see the "bad ozone" with your eyes, but we can see the effects of this bad ozone on certain items such as a rubber band.

Materials Needed:

~ 3 glass jars
~ 3 medium size rubber bands

~ magnifying glass
~ Pen

Ready To Go? Let's Head Out!

~ Place a rubber band around the center of each glass jar. (The rubber band should not stretch too much. The results of this activity will be altered if the rubber band is stretched too greatly.)

~ Write the date and location on a piece of paper and place it in your jar.

~ Examine a section of your rubber band with a magnifying glass. Draw what you observe. Mark this section with a pen.

~ Place one jar outside in the shade, away from the direct sunlight. Place one jar on the kitchen counter. And, if at all possible, place one jar near a copy machine. (If you don't have a copy machine, perhaps you can receive permission to place your jar near a copy machine at the library or church office?) (Most copy machines use an electrostatic charging of a cylinder in the copying process. The accompanying ionization creates ozone—so placing your jar with the rubber band near a copy machine will make for a more interesting experiment.)

~ Every day for a week, examine your rubber bands with your magnifying glass. Write down your observations and sketch what you see happening. Can you see the effects of "bad ozone"?
Be a detective and hunt down the answers to these queries!

~ Is your rubber band cracking? Or pitting?

~ At which location did your rubber band show the greatest change?

~ And at which location did your rubber change the least?

~ On which day did you see the first noticeable changes?

~ Did all the rubber bands change on the same day?

~ What do you think caused the changes of the rubber bands? (Ozone will deteriorate the rubber bands at a rate dependent upon the ozone levels in the surrounding air.)

28

Too-Fun-to-Resist Excursion!

HAVE A SPECTACULAR SHOWER!

Here is a shower where you will need no shampoo or a towel! Nor will you need to trek up through the atmosphere until you reach the mesosphere.

Instead of freezing way up there in the mesosphere, why not head outside for the best shower of all—a shower of meteors!

Late autumn, especially mid-October to mid-December, is the prime season of meteor showers, when God dazzles with brilliant flashes of streaking light in the night sky. And you won't want to miss it!

Ready To Go? Let's Head Out!

The only materials you will need for this too-fun-to-resist activity is perhaps a warm cup of hot chocolate to sip while standing out there under the night sky, and a blanket to snuggle in! (And, of course, a fellow geographer to share the wonder with!)

Dates of meteor showers are listed at the International Meteor Organization Website:

http://www.imo.net/calendar

Write the appropriate dates on your calendar so you won't forget!

Set your alarm clock for the hushed hours of dark before sunrise. You can observe many more meteors near dawn than after dusk.

If you want the best seat to view a meteor shower, find the darkest location possible. Any man-made lights should be avoided if you are seeking a great showing of God's lights.

As all world-travelers do, take along your camera to capture God's wonders!

And remember: By sky gazing at meteor showers, you are actually seeing God's marvels up in the mesosphere—without even leaving your own backyard!

"And as I looked, behold, a storm wind was coming from the north, a great cloud with fire flashing continually and a bright light around it, and in its midst something like glowing metal in the midst of the fire."
(Ezekiel 1:4)

FALLING THROUGH THE SKY

Chapter 3

This morning, when you awoke, did you crawl out from under a cozy thermal blanket? When I was a child, we lived in a very old house, and in the winter I used to wake up to *snow* sprinkled on my thermal blankets!   I'd slip out of bed to the icy cold floor, and wonder how low the thermometer had plunged during the frosty night!   Do you have a thermostat in your home to control the temperature? Where I lived as a child, there was no thermostat in our house to turn up to take the chill out of the air. We just had to stoke the wood up in the fireplace and wait for the warmth of the flames to heat up our old farmhouse. Before I headed out the door to school, my mother often would pack steaming soup into my orange thermos bottle. In that thermos bottle, my soup would stay warm until I slurped it down during my lunch hour—so then I would be warm too!

Did you notice all the words that began with "*therm*" during my morning? As noted geographers and fine detectives, have you discovered what the root word "*therme*" means?   Yes! "***Therme***" means "heat" in the Greek language. So words that contain "*therm*" refer to how hot something is. Well, fellow-geographers, would you like to explore part of the Earth's atmosphere called the **thermosphere,** a place that is sizzling hot—but is NOT!   If you are eager to experience a very strange adventure, let's head out into the Earth's Upper Atmosphere!

Geographers often refer to a map to remember where they have been and to plot where they are going. So let's pull out ours and recall the sights of the Lower Atmosphere. First we hiked through the ***troposphere***, the layer of the atmosphere in which we live and where our weather occurs. Here we discovered the higher we traveled, the nippier our noses became! Then we headed up through the ***stratosphere***, the layer in the atmosphere that actually got *warmer* as we traveled higher. (That was because of the *ozone* layer netting ultraviolet radiation from the sun, remember?) Then we found ourselves in the ***mesosphere*** where we were again wrapping our scarves tighter in the bone-chilling temperatures, but we were still peeking out from behind our scarves in search of falling stars!

That is where we have traveled to this point in the Earth's atmosphere. What adventures lie ahead? Let's wave farewell to the mesosphere and the Earth's Lower atmosphere, and set off to discover the thermosphere of the **Upper Atmosphere**!

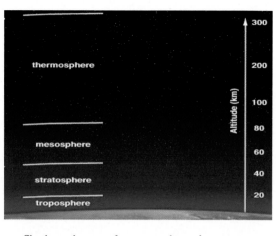

Check out the map of our atmosphere adventures—so where are we?   *NASA*

The **thermosphere** extends to 370 miles (600 km.) above our earth home. That means if you were driving in your car straight up, you would have left home after breakfast and it would now be mid-afternoon! That's a long time traveling straight up!

The thermosphere indeed lives up to its name. (Remember that "*therme*" comes from the Greek word "heat" so thermosphere means "heat sphere.") The higher we climb into the thermosphere, the higher the temperature climbs too! Actually, the temperature hikes so high, it is hard even to imagine—as high as 3,000 degrees F (1,700 degrees C)!! Why does the temperature keep climbing? The temperature spikes higher because we are climbing closer towards the Earth's source of heat, the sun.

You are probably thinking now might be good time to peel off your winter gear of scarf and mittens. Not too fast! If you exposed your skin to the thermosphere, you actually wouldn't feel hot in the least! Not even at those dizzyingly high temperatures! You would actually feel VERY cold! Isn't that puzzling?

Have you ever sat in a dark, cold room in front of a light bulb? The temperature of the light bulb would be very hot indeed. You would get burned if you wrapped your fingers around that glowing light bulb. However, since there is only one light bulb in the room, you would still be feeling pretty nippy!

The thermosphere is like that large, black room. The molecules floating around in the thermosphere are like only a few light bulbs in an enormous, empty arena. Those molecules are very, VERY hot, but there simply isn't very many of them! So you would be feeling cold in the thermosphere since there would not be enough molecules bumping into your skin to actually make your skin feel warm!

Temperature actually measures how fast molecules are moving in the air around us. The molecules up here in the thermosphere are moving with incredible speed. Thus the temperature of the thermosphere reads high. But there just isn't that many molecules way up in the thermosphere! So while the temperature reads high, our skins feel bitingly cold!

Isn't it rather absurd that up here in the thermosphere, the "heat sphere," closer to the blazing sun, we would be shivering? The thermosphere is where it is hot—but it is NOT!

As thermosphere tourists, we would have more serious concerns than merely feeling frosty! Recall that the ozone layer is way *below* us in the stratosphere. It is that ozone layer that protects people on our home of Earth from harmful ultraviolet radiation from the sun. In the thermosphere we are not well defended from the sun's radiation. While we may think it a bit amusing that we would be *cold* up here in this "*heat* sphere," we wouldn't find this severe dose of ultraviolet radiation amusing in the least! (Then again, we *are* just imagining what it would be like if you really *could* take a walking tour through the earth's atmosphere!)

Tell the folks at home all about it!

*Let's take a wee rest here on our walking tour. Tell us, where have we been? What lies above the mesosphere? (**Memory Joggers**: What does thermosphere mean and how far does it extend above Earth? What would it feel like to walk through the thermosphere—and why? What else would be happening to us up in the thermosphere because the ozone layer is below us in the stratosphere?) Now that we are feeling refreshed, let's head out again!*

Doesn't the Aurora Borealis, or Northern Lights, shine magnificent above Alaska? God's love lights are breathtaking, reminding us of the ionosphere that protects our Earth!

As the stratosphere has a layer within it called the ozone layer, the thermosphere has a layer within it called the **ionosphere**. God also created the ionosphere in the thermosphere to protect our Earthly home.

If someone were pelting you with fiery darts, wouldn't you grab a shield to defend yourself? Well, the ionosphere is a unique shield that God created for

Earth. There are explosions happening on the surface of the sun called "solar flares." Searing hot particles from the sun fling out into space at speeds over a million kilometers per hour! Even at such terrific speeds, these particles take two to three days to reach our atmosphere! And when these sun particles, these ions, come charging towards our home, our shield of the ionosphere defends Earth.

Did you know that from certain places on our Earth, on late, dark nights, you can actually see the ionosphere shielding Earth from these deadly particles? When these particles from the sun smash into the ionosphere, the collision creates the most glorious glowing lights—like fireworks way up in the ionosphere!

Have you ever lit off fireworks? Maybe you sit in a park on national holidays and gaze up at cascading fireworks to show your love for the country you live in. In my family, we also light off fireworks when we want to celebrate our love for each other! We shoot off these "love lights" into the sky to show our love on wedding days or days when little babies are born or on birthdays!

Well, the fireworks up in the ionosphere are *God's* love lights to all of us who live on Earth. These stunning love lights, called an **aurora**, are a result of the ionosphere shielding Earth from deadly sun particles. If these dangerous sun particles reached our home, we could not live on this planet. Thus, the next time you see a breathtaking aurora, red and green lights fluttering like a shimmering curtain in the night sky, remember how much God loves all of us on Earth! Thankfully, He created the ionosphere to protect the home He loves and made for us.

When you see fireworks explode overhead, do you "ooohh" and "aaahhh"? When people gaze upon God's love lights of auroras up in the ionosphere, the glorious sight captivates them too! Auroras are most easily seen in the northern and southern regions of Earth; that is why they are often called the "Northern Lights" and "Southern Lights." One famous Northern poet, Robert Service, wrote this poem of wonder describing an aurora:

[T]he skies of night were alive with light...,
They were rose and silver shod;
It was not good for the eyes of man —
'Twas a sight for the eyes of God.

Some believe that the prophet Ezekiel in the Bible was the first person to ever write down a description of an aurora. Ezekiel wrote **"And as I looked, behold, a storm wind was coming from the north, a great cloud with fire flashing continually and a bright light around it, and in its midst something like glowing metal in the midst of the fire."** (Eze. 1:4) Do you think Ezekiel may have seen God's love lights, an aurora?

What would an aurora look like if you were up in the ionosphere during one of these clashes between bullet-fast sun particles and the gases in the ionosphere? You'd notice a faint glow all around. People who study the atmosphere think standing in an aurora up in the ionosphere would be a bit like standing in a rainbow—which is another love sign from God, isn't it?!

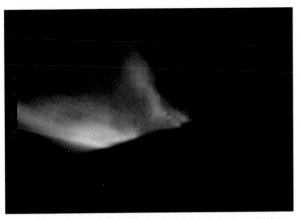

The dancing aurora borealis dazzles in the night sky! *NASA*

Tell the folks at home all about it!

*Tell us what you know about the layer that lies within the thermosphere. (**Memory Joggers**: Why did God create the ionosphere? What happens when particles from the sun collide with the ionosphere? Why do we call an aurora "love lights"? Describe an aurora.)*
Let's move on!

As tourists of the atmosphere, wandering through the thermosphere and ionosphere, we are a long way from our home of Earth. Have you ever been a long way from home? I was once a long way from home for a long time in a place where everyone spoke a different language than I did. And I became sick—homesick. Homesick is a peculiar word because it does *not* mean that you are sick of your home. It means that you are sick because you are *away* from your beloved home. And in that far away land, I was sick because I missed my home so badly.

Do you know what cured my homesickness? The ionosphere cured my homesickness! Far from home, I would wake in the wee, dark hours of the morning. Tiptoeing out of bed, I would quietly turn on my radio. Do you know what I would hear? I could hear the voices of people, speaking my language, who lived near my home! Even though my home was many hundreds and hundreds of miles away! It was the ionosphere that allowed me to hear those dearly loved voices from home!

The ionosphere has layers of particles, called ions, which reflect radio signals. The radio station in my hometown sent out radio waves. Those radio waves bumped into those ion layers in the ionosphere, and returned to Earth, much like you bounce a rubber ball. The waves then bounced again up to the ionosphere and returned to earth. Those radio waves kept bouncing and bumping, bouncing and bumping, from earth to the ionosphere—all the way to me—that homesick kid in that far away place. The ionosphere brought me a little bit of home in those radio waves and I wasn't so homesick anymore!

If there were no ionosphere, the radio waves would have left my hometown radio station and just drifted off into space. If there were no ionosphere, there would be pretty much radio silence! If there were no ionosphere, I would have been one *very* homesick kid with no voices from home to listen to!

(But why did I have to wake up in the middle of the night to hear that radio station from my hometown? Well, when the sun goes down, changes happen in the ionosphere. Those changes allow some radio waves to then bounce further along. So that is why late at night you might turn on your radio and hear voices from hundreds and hundreds of miles away! It is all because of the way God created the ionosphere!)

Weren't there many sights to marvel at here in the thermosphere where the ionosphere is? Hold onto those memories of auroras and radios so we later can tell our tales!

We are almost finished touring the Earth's atmosphere. Our final stop is the **exosphere**. The exosphere lies beyond 300 to 620 miles (500-1000 km.) away from Earth. The exosphere is the utmost layer of the atmosphere, like the outer skin of an onion.

We have a box in our house that just stores onions. If you peeked inside our onion box, you'd find the bottom of the box covered with outer onion skins that have just fallen off their onions.

Something similar happens in the exosphere. **Exo** means *"out of"* in Greek. And up in the exosphere, lighter molecules escape *out of* the atmosphere and drift off into space, a bit like onion skins peeling off the onion!

But be careful that *you* don't escape out of the Earth's atmosphere as we travel through the exosphere. Once you leave the exosphere, you have left the blanket of air swaddling Earth which is our atmosphere... and you are wandering out into outer space! As lighter molecules can escape out of the exosphere, you too would be feeling lighter and lighter and could easily drift off!

Tell the folks at home all about it!

How might the ionosphere comfort a homesick kid?
*(**Memory Joggers**: What do ions in the ionosphere reflect? Can you describe how radio waves travel? What would happen if God had not created the ionosphere? Why can you hear radio stations from further away at night?) What does "exosphere" mean and what happens in the exosphere?*

As we have come to the end of our atmospheric journey, now would be a good time to return to Earth—before *you* float off into outer space! Ready to drift back down through the curtains of air wrapped around our home?

Here we go! Down through the **exosphere** (don't want you to soar out of the atmosphere!)... falling now through the **ionosphere** layer (see God's love lights? Hear the radio stations?)...now back down through the rest of the **thermosphere** (feeling hot—but NOT!?)...falling now down into the **mesosphere** (catch a glimpse of any meteors over the scarf wrapped around your face?)...tumbling now back to the stratosphere (stay out of the ozone net!), and finally into the **troposphere**...where we plunk down onto a storm cloud!

We've fully explored the curtains of air draped around Earth called our atmosphere! And now that we've inspected the curtains shrouding our home, don't you marvel at the God who **"stretches out the heavens as a curtain"** (Isa. 40:22)! Aren't you eager to draw back the curtains and take a peek into the rooms of our home, Earth! But don't peek just yet—that is our *next* tour!

POSTCARD HOME

As you catch your breath from today's Upper Atmosphere tour, why don't you jot down what you've seen on your postcard-size piece of cardstock? Sketch a picture on the front of your postcard of the different stops you made through the Upper Atmosphere (can you remember them all?) Then write a vivid letter about the amazing, nearly unbelievable, things you've seen as an atmospheric tourist! Now punch a hole in your postcard and put it on your ring! This is one trip you'll want to remember!

(Postcard templates are available on the CD-ROM in the back of your book)

Reaching Out
to His World

Look at a radio in your home. Did you know that for many people living around the world that a radio is like their Bible? The voice that speaks through their radio tells them about the love of God! **Trans-World Radio** is an organization that broadcasts the gospel in over 190 languages all over the world! And they rely on the ionosphere to do it!

Using short waves aimed at the ionosphere, the radio signal is bounced from one point on Earth to another—all around this planet, 24 hours a day! A radio wave beam enters the ionosphere, the ionosphere "bends" it—and sends it back to Earth! Since the ionosphere changes in height and density, Trans-World Radio short-wave radio broadcasts are heard differently at different times of day. And for millions of people living in non-Christian countries, the ionosphere sending those radio waves of God's love into their homes, has changed their lives!

So **what can you do to reach out** to God's world using the radio? You can help support a ministry like Trans-World Radio!

- Pray right now for Trans-World Radio! That God would continue to use people, radios—and the ionosphere—to bring many more people into the family of faith!

- Check out Trans-World Radio's website and read the online diaries of people who are missionaries using the radio to share the Good News! http://www.twr.org

- Subscribe to their free magazine and read how radio is taking the love of God all around the world!

Aren't you thankful for the ionosphere?

Further Explorations

The Northern Lights *by Lucy Jago*

(For older students) An exceptionally well-written work, this book chronicles the life of Kristian Birkeland and his quest to understand the aurora borealis. An intriguing tale of a little-known, extraordinary man who led a life full of intellectual and physical adventures. Take up the adventures with Birkeland!

Northern lights *by D.M. Souza*

(Read aloud to younger students, independent reading for Gr. 4-6) Large, mysterious pictures of skies in dazzling light and color accompany Souza text, explaining the action of solar-wind particles, magnetic fields, and atmospheric gases in common terms, relating difficult ideas to occurrences familiar to young people. A glossary, a folklore section of interesting facts, and specific details of the how and when of auroras rounds out this volume.

Auroras : light shows in the night sky *by Donna Walsh Shepherd*

(Read independently Gr.3-5) What are auroras? Where are they found? How do they occur? This book answers these queries and more. Beginning with the story of a young Alaskan Native boy recalling various legends and stories his grandmother has told him about the auroral lights in the Arctic sky, weaving other tales from around the world of how people have tried to explain the phenomena and scientific discoveries.

The Radio *by Gayle Worland*

(Gr. 2-4) Who is Guglielmo Marconi? He has nothing to do with macaroni! In 1901, he became the first person to send radio signals over a long distance. Explore the history of the radio, and discover how this great invention developed into the radios we use today. (Includes directions on how to create your own radio waves!)

Too-Fun-to-Resist Excursion!

MAKE A MODEL OF THE ATMOSPHERE!

God created our atmosphere with us in mind! With just the right amount of oxygen in the troposphere, with the layer of ozone in the stratosphere, the meteor showers in the mesosphere, the shield of the ionosphere in the thermosphere and finally the exiting of the exosphere, our atmosphere perfectly allows us to live on this planet! Why not make a model of the atmosphere so you can show folks the wisdom of our Creator God?

Materials Needed:

~ the most narrow glass jar or cup you can find
(it must be able to hold 1000 ml or 1 qt)
~ white flour
~ white sugar
~ brown sugar

~ yellow cornmeal
~ measuring cup
~ small white labels or sections of masking tape

Ready To Go? Let's Head Out!

(Now, please keep in mind that these are relative proportions and not exact points of departure for the individual layers of the atmosphere.)

~ Measure out 1 tablespoon (15 ml) of white flour. Pour it into your jar and lightly shake your jar so that the flour is lying evenly on the bottom of the jar. Write "Troposphere" on your small label or section of masking tape and stick it on your glass jar where the white flour lies.

~ Now measure out 3 tablespoons (45 ml) of brown sugar. Pour it carefully into your jar, over top of the layer of white flour. Gently even out this layer in your jar. Write "Stratosphere" on your small label or section of masking tape and stick it on your glass jar where the brown sugar lies.

~ Next measure out 3 tablespoons (45 ml) of yellow cornmeal. Again, pour this into your jar, creating a layer of yellow over your brown sugar layer. Even this layer out. Label this layer "Mesosphere."

~ Finally, measure out 3 cups (895 ml) of white sugar and pour it into your jar. Gently shake your jar to even out this layer. Write "Thermosphere" on your small label or section of masking tape and stick it on your glass jar where the white sugar lies.

There! You've just created a model of our atmosphere! Now, can you find someone to show how God created such grand curtains for our Earthly home!

Too-Fun-to-Resist Excursion!

TURN THE RADIO ON!

Do you recall what layer of the atmosphere allows us to listen to the radio? You cannot see the ionosphere—but you could *listen* to the effects of the ionosphere!

Materials:
~ an AM radio

~ a map of your region or state or province

Ready To Go? Let's Head Out!

~ Turn on your radio and open your atlases. Locate the most distant station you can hear and its distance in miles from your home.

~ Then select a location on the band on the low end (between 540 AM and 640 AM) that is *between* stations. (That is, you will not be hearing an actual station.) What kind of noises do you hear? Write down in a journal the times when noises change and the various kinds of noises. If you hear occasional pops and crackles, that is an indication of a lightning storm. Humming and buzzing would be due to electronic noise.

~ The make-up of the ionosphere changes near sunset and sunrise. And even though you cannot see the ionosphere, you can hear those changes! Near sunset or sunrise there may be a sudden change in the volume of background noise. Far-away, distant stations may now be heard! Can you be a good detective and note the time of these changes? Can you find the location of these far-away stations on your map?

Your radio has just let you listen into the invisible changes in the ionosphere!

"With whom did He consult and who gave Him understanding?
And who taught Him the path of justice and taught Him knowledge,
and informed Him of the way of understanding?
Behold, the nations are like a drop from a bucket,
and are regarded as a speck of dust on the scales;
behold He lifts up the islands like fine dust."

Isaiah 40: 14-15

PUZZLE DIRECTIONS

Chapter 4

(Grab an atlas or a globe to take along with you on this journey!)

I once ate a puzzle. A very delicious puzzle it was. Rather than chewing on some dry cardboard shapes, I sunk my teeth into... a cookie puzzle of gingerbread! When all the gingerbread puzzle pieces were locked together, a heart shape appeared with the name *"Jesus!"* written across the golden brown cookie! It was the best-tasting puzzle I have ever assembled!

But even that lip-smacking puzzle may not compare to the wondrous pieces we geographers are going to puzzle with today!

Do you remember imagining what Earth looked like from a space rocket? Since we've already explored the curtain of air that is draped around Earth, our grand atmosphere adventures, why don't you crowd in to get a good peek into the rooms of our home?

What do you see through the spacecraft window? (If you could place a globe of the world in front of you, that would be like looking at the Earth from space.) Do you see a brilliantly blue ball with some strangely shaped puzzle pieces glued about it? What are those odd shapes? Yes, those pieces are stretches of dry land. (Can you figure out the names of these two pieces of dry land? Look on your globe. The answer is tucked at the very end of this chapter.)

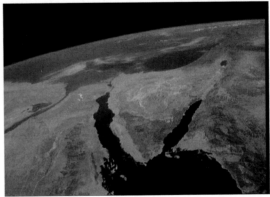

From your space-side seat, can you identify these puzzle shapes on Earth's surface? *NASA*

Much like rooms in your own home, those pieces of dry land each has its own name. I once knew of a home with rooms named the *"Sugar Mountain Room"* (that was the name of the mountain that loomed outside the room's window), and the *"Fairie Belle Room"* (that was the name of the little girl who lived in that home). But the rooms of dry land on our home of Earth—the rooms where we all live—have very different names.

Geographers obviously do not call the shapes of land on Earth "puzzles pieces" or "rooms" but refer to them as "**continents.**" The word "**continent**" comes from the Latin word "**continens**" which means "*continuous* mass of land." Peering down from our space-shuttle window, those "rooms" on our Earth home are large continuous masses of land, aren't they?

This is a map of Earth's continents of land. Can you name them all?

Now that we know the rooms in our home are called "continents," come in close for a better look at those puzzle pieces!

From your perch in space, can you gaze down at a continent shaped like a face? Well, the name of the continent Europe comes from the Greek words *"Eurys"* (broad) and *"Ops"* (face). Do you think this puzzle piece looks like someone with a broad face or big eyes? (Think of the Black Sea and the Baltic Sea as Europe's two large eyes. After you find her eyes, where do you think broad-faced, wide-eyed Europe's nose and chin are?)

Used by Permission: Donna Ritchie

Can you hear the waves lapping up on the coastline of Nice, France on the continent of Europe? (Nice is pronounced "Neece"—-but spelled "Nice". Nice, yes?)

In Greek mythology, Europa was a beautiful Phoenician princess. One day, so the Greeks say, while Europa was gathering flowers by the sea, a white bull lay down in front of her. Europa carefully slid onto its back. Then, like a flash of lightning, the bull charged off, plunging into the sea. Greek myth claims that the bull carried wide-eyed Europa off to the continent we now call Europe. (Your eyes may have grown wide too if a wild bull bolted off with you clinging behind!) Think of Europe as the puzzle piece of the lovely, wide-eyed lady, pitching about in the sea!

Europe really is the continent splashing about in the water! Europe's land juts and zigzags back and forth by the sea, much like that bull probably darted and dashed with wide-eyed Europa on its back! The continent of Europe may be small, but its coastline, the land that meets the water, is longer than other continents that are THREE times bigger than Europe!

Like two puzzle pieces locked together, wide-eyed, water-splashing Europe is linked to another continent called *"Asia."* If you listen to the Greek myths, they say *"Asia"* was a water fairy that rained water down on earth. But since we know the truth that God alone pours water out on the face of the Earth (Amos 9:6), we'll leave the Greeks to their fairytales. The word "Asia" is actually thought to have derived from the ancient Assyrian word "**asu**," meaning that Asia is the *"land of the sunrise."* Asia may have the shortest name of all the continents, but it is the largest of all the continents. Like the sun is the largest body in our solar system, Asia has more land, more people and more kinds of animals and plants than any other continent! With more than 17 million square miles of land, and over 3.8 billion people (like the ones here in Shanghai, China), Asia, the land of the rising sun, is an immense continent! Think of Asia as a massive sun. Can you picture wide-eye Europe watching the sunrise of enormous Asia?

Used with Permission: ManYee DeSandees

Asia makes up more than 1/3 of Earth's land surface and over half of Earth's family lives on the continent of Asia.

Tell the folks at home all about it!

*What can you tell us about the continents of Earth? What picture do you have in your mind when you think Europe and Asia? (**Memory Joggers**: What does the word "**continent**" mean? What does the name "**Europe**" mean? What is the story of Europa from Greek mythology? Can you share anything else you discovered about Europe? What does "**Asia**" mean?)*

Looking down from our space-side seats, you may be able to see wide-eyed Europe almost touching another continent of land. Europe here almost touches the large room to its south. This room south of Europe is the continent "**Africa.**" It is possible that "Africa" comes from the Latin word "**Aprica**," meaning "basking in the sun." Can you see that Africa is shaped like a zebra's head, nose pointing downwards (South Africa), ear jutting out (Somalia), eye blinking (Lake Victoria)? So, think of Africa as the zebra basking in the sun!

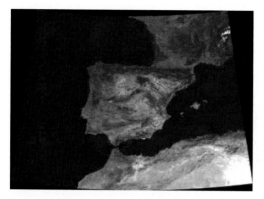

Actually, a zebra wouldn't be the only animal basking in the sun in Africa! There are more different kinds of hoofed animals in Africa than on any other continent! Two billion birds also fly every winter from colder continents to the continent of Africa to bask in its warm sunshine. When you think of Africa, can you envision the lovely wide-eyed lady, Europe, riding the zebra of Africa, both basking in the sunrise of Asia?

Europe and Africa nearly touch—
-here at the Strait of Gibraltar, the 2
continents are only 8 miles (13 km) apart!
NASA

If you press your forehead against the glass of the space-shuttle window, do you catch a glimpse of another continent dangling under rising Asia? It is the smallest puzzle-piece continent on our Earth home...but it has the longest name of all the continents: "Australia." The word "***Australia***" comes from the Latin word "***auster***" which means "southern wind." Do you think Australia looks like a cloud blowing in on a southern wind?

Used by permission: Steve Canipe

Africa is not only one of the richest
continents in resources like
diamonds, copper and gold,
It has a rich diversity of animal life,
such as this herd of zebras!

If you lived in Australia, you *would* be looking for a cloud blowing in on a southern wind! Australia is a dry continent, as you can see in this picture of the Uluhru Rock taken in Australia's "outback." Over one-third of the continent is a desert land of little rain and another one third of the continent is a semi-desert grassland. Folks in Australia don't wait for a cloud blowing in on a southern wind to bring some water—they just live along the coastline next to the ocean instead!

Can you see in your mind's eye the picture our puzzle is making? Envision a cloud blowing in on a southern wind (that's Australia) as a brilliant sun rises (Asia) over lovely, wide-eyed Europe, resting on the basking zebra of Africa.

Used by permission: Steve Canipe

Australia is hot and flat, just like a
frying pan—with Uluhru Rock rising
out of its outback.

Tell the folks at home all about it!

Tell me what you discovered about Africa and Australia! (**Memory Joggers**: *What does the name "**Africa**" mean? What does the name "**Australia**" mean? What picture do you have in your mind when you think of Europe, Asia, Africa and Australia?*)

Are these four continents the only ones on our Earth home? Well, if you fluffed your pillow and snuggled in for a long, long nap up there beside your space-shuttle window, you'd wake up to find those four continents gone! Two new puzzle shapes glued to the blue ball of Earth would be looking back at you! What happened?

Have you ever watched a very talented person whirl a basketball around on his finger? And the ball spins and spins and spins?

When God made the Earth by the word of His mouth, He gave the Earth a little nudge...and it has been spinning ever since! Every 24 hours the Earth spins completely around. This is how God makes day and night for us on Earth! For 12 hours, one half of the sphere of Earth is facing the sun...then that half rotates away from the sun into darkness and night....while the other half of sphere of Earth stretches and warms in the sun!

I am not sure how fast someone can twirl a basketball on a finger, but would you like to guess how fast the Earth is spinning? The Earth is spinning around at 1,000 miles (1,600 km.) per hour! Surprisingly, no one on Earth is even dizzy, are we?

In the beginning, God created the heavens and the earth...simply by the breathtaking words of His mouth. *NASA*

Think of the sun as a lamp and our Earth as the ball. The side of the ball facing the lamp is like the side of our Earth facing the sun---while the other side sleeps in darkness!

47

Now this might make you dizzy: not only is Earth like a spinning basketball, the Earth is also spinning around the sun! Hard to imagine, isn't it? Picture in your mind the basketball pro spinning his basketball on his finger (that is Earth) as he walks in a big, wide circle around and around and around you (pretending that you are the sun). While we sit here on this spinning Earth, which is spinning around the sun, we are traveling many, many miles through space! While you have read this page, Earth just traveled more than 1,000 miles (1, 600 km) in its nearly circular trip around the sun! If the Lord grants you 70 years of life, you will have traveled *41 billion miles* (66 billion km.) in space as the spinning Earth spins around the sun! You may not know it, but you are a first-class traveler of the universe just sitting in your back yard!

God, the Master Builder, made no errors when creating our home called Earth by the word of His mouth. If God had made the Earth to spin slower, those folks on the side of the Earth facing the sun would become blistering hot, while those on the side of Earth facing away from the sun would be chattering their teeth in the biting cold. What if God spun our Earth faster than 1,000 miles (1,600 km) an hour? Then you'd really have to hold on to your hat! Because then all of us would experience fierce, violent winds that would make life very, very difficult.

Tell the folks at home all about it!

Tell me about our spinning Earth! (**Memory Joggers**: *What makes night and day for us on Earth? How fast is the Earth spinning? What would happen if God had not spun our world so perfectly?*)

While you were dozing up there by the rocket window, God perfectly rotated the Earth. The planet has spun so that Australia, Asia, Europe and Africa are now tucked into their beds, sleeping in the cool dark. And guess who is awake, playing in the sunshine? All the people on the two *other* puzzle shapes!

Do you see those two continents down there? These two puzzle shapes are *not* named after some imaginary women of Greek myth.   These two continents are named "North and South America"—and they are named after a baby boy!

"**Amerigo**" was the name an Italian mama picked for her baby boy! Little Amerigo Vespucci grew up and sailed away from that continent of wide-eyed Europe and right around our ball of Earth—until he bumped into these two new puzzle pieces. Now, some sailors had pulled their boats up on these landmasses and thought they were on the far sides of the continent of Asia. But Amerigo thought differently. He thought these were different puzzle pieces entirely, completely different landmasses. Amerigo did not think the boats had run into Asia at all—but *new continents*! Amerigo Vespucci was the first person to call these landmasses the "New World." So the continents, "**North and South America,**" are named after that boy, Amerigo!

It might be said that North and South America themselves are like two boys, brothers, in fact. Don't all brothers share—and not just their toys, but they also share the same parents, the same house, and sometimes even the same clothes. Well, North and South America share many things in common too! Both North and South America have remarkable waters. North America has the world's largest concentration of fresh waters: the Great Lakes...and South America has world's mightiest river, the Amazon. Both North and South America have native peoples who were wrongly named Indians by a man who thought he had met people from India! Both North and South America had people from Europe come form settlements on their continents. Both continents have nearly the same number of people living on them. Why North and South America are even attached to each other—by a skinny piece of land called Central America!

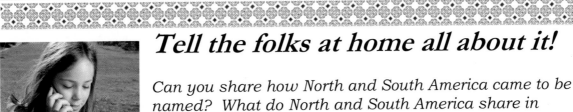

Tell the folks at home all about it!

Can you share how North and South America came to be named? What do North and South America share in common?

Now, your home may have a front side, facing the street, and a backside, facing out to your backyard. Although Earth doesn't really have a front or backside at all, geographers have termed a name for each half of the ball of Earth. "**Hemisphere**" is the Latin word for "*half ball.*" The side of our planet with the south wind blowing (Australia) as the sun rises (Asia) over lovely wide-eyed Europe on the sun-basking zebra of Africa—this side of our Earth ball is called the "**Eastern**

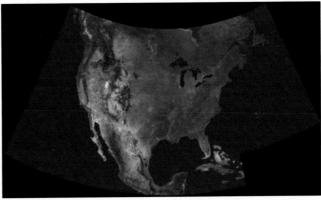

North America has the longest coastline of any continent, 96,000 miles (154,497,000 km.) long! *NASA*

Hemisphere." The side of the ball of earth with the two "boy-named" continents, North and South America, are in the "***Western Hemisphere.***"

The Earth is also divided in half, right around its waist, by an invisible line called the ***equator***. If you trace the invisible line of the equator around your globe, maybe you felt your finger getting hot? If you did, that is because the belt of the equator is the hottest part of our Earth, dividing our planet exactly in half. Above the equator is the "top half ball," the ***Northern Hemisphere***. (The Northern Hemisphere has the North Pole poking out the very peak of its half.) And below the equator, is the "bottom half ball," the "***Southern Hemisphere.***" (And what is poking out at its peak? Yes, the South Pole!)

You may have missed one puzzle piece—because it isn't in just the Eastern Hemisphere or the Western Hemisphere. This continent is in *both* the Eastern and Western hemispheres—and most of it is hiding under a mile thick sheet of ice! Have you ever been to the end of the world? If you pick up your globe and look under South America or Australia, to the South Pole, you will find what some people call the end of the world—the seventh continent, "***Antarctica.***"

The name "**Antarctica**" comes from the Greek, meaning "*opposite the bear.*" Looking at the sky in the north, the Greeks thought they saw a group of stars that made the shape of "***arktos,***" meaning, "*bear.*" "**Antarctica**" lies in the opposite direction of this northern shape of stars, so it is "opposite the bear." So, remember the continent at the *southern* end of the world is Antarctica, opposite the bear!

Antarctica certainly is opposite or different than any other continent on Earth. Unlike any other continent, there are no cities, no rivers, and very few animals or plants. That is because Antarctica is so very frigid! The very *warmest* day of the year in the Antarctica is colder than your freezer! (-5 to –31 F or –15 to –35C) But the penguins, seals and whales like it!

Tell the folks at home all about it!

Put in your own words what you've just discovered!
(**Memory Joggers**: *How is Earth divided? What continents are in the Eastern Hemisphere? What continents are in the Western Hemisphere? What divides the Northern Hemisphere from the Southern Hemisphere? Tell me what you remember about Antarctica!*)

Has anyone ever tied a kerchief around your eyes then spun you around several times? You likely then stumbled off in one direction while everyone giggled. When they untied the bandana, wasn't it a surprise to discover that you had not headed in the direction you had intended but had bumbled off in another direction entirely? People say that when you are lost, "You've gotten yourself all turned around"—which is exactly what happened to you when they blindfolded you and spun you around! So, how do you NOT get all turned around? How do you know which direction is which on our Earth home?

Can you find the window where the sun first beams its rays into your house while you are eating breakfast? Now point towards that window with your right hand (maybe that is the hand you write with?). You will be pointing East, for the sun rises in the **EAST**. (Here's a riddle that I am certain that you clever geographers can now puzzle together: why is the half of Earth where Asia lies called the *Eastern* Hemisphere? Ah, you are right! Remember that Asia comes from the word "*asu*" that means "land of the sunrise"? The sun *rises* first over Asia on our Earthly home. So where Asia lies is called the *Eastern* Hemisphere!)

Keep your finger pointing in the direction of East, where the sun rises. If you hold out your other hand, you will be pointing **WEST.** *West* is the direction where the sunsets. (And North and South America lie in the *Western* Hemisphere because they are the land of the setting sun.) Don't grow too tired holding your arms out to the East and West! If your right hand is pointing towards the sunrise, East—then your nose is aiming **NORTH**! And the direction **SOUTH** lies hidden right behind you. There you go! You have just solved the mystery of which direction is which. If you remember the word "*NEWS*"—nose pointing North, then right hand East, left hand West and South sneaking behind—you'll remember each direction. And you will have learned the skill of directions that every geographer needs to know to get around our Earth home!

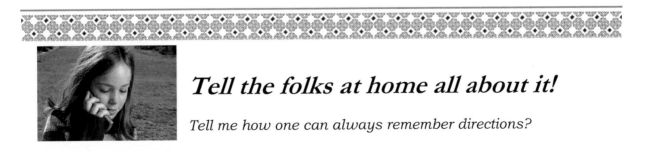

Tell the folks at home all about it!

Tell me how one can always remember directions?

Have you ever carefully worked with intense concentration and diligence on a complicated puzzle, when your little brother or sister reached out a small hand to swiftly scramble up all the puzzle pieces? Well, come close to examine the Earth's puzzle pieces very closely. Do you think that at one time "the boys" of North and South America were not separated from wide-eyed Europa and basking Africa? Is it possible that some continental puzzle pieces were once fitted together....but have now shifted and moved?

As you ponder on how God may have incredibly shuffled around the puzzle pieces of our continents (that's a coming adventure), why don't you give your globe one final spin for today? Marvel at the fact that only God can spin our Earth like a big ball—or make any dry land—or command the sun to rise in the East and set in the West! God knows exactly where you are—even in the middle of the night. For God alone has

Antarctica is the coldest, driest, windiest, and least populated of all the continents on Earth. Covered with nearly a mile (1.6 km) of ice, melting all the ice of Antarctica would raise the Earth's oceans by 200 ft. (61 m.), flooding cities all over the world! (Remember, your Dad is likely around 6 ft. tall (1.82 m) — so 200 ft. (61 m.) would be like 33 Dads standing on top of each other— and THAT is how much the oceans would rise if all the ice in Antarctica melted!)

the Whole World—all seven continents and every one of us—in His hands. So *each* of us, *everywhere* in this home of Earth, are in VERY good hands indeed!

POSTCARD HOME

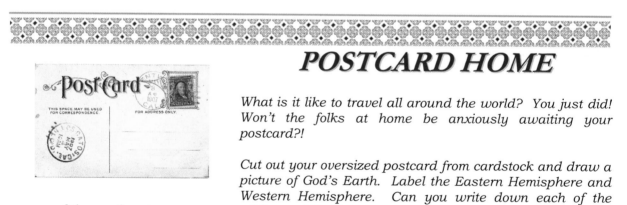

What is it like to travel all around the world? You just did! Won't the folks at home be anxiously awaiting your postcard?!

Cut out your oversized postcard from cardstock and draw a picture of God's Earth. Label the Eastern Hemisphere and Western Hemisphere. Can you write down each of the names of the continents on your map of the world? Now turn your postcard over and write about your favorite pit stop—which was your favorite continent? What did you discover about that unique continent? And to think that God formed each continent with his own hands! **Psalms 95:5... and his hands formed the dry land.**

(Postcard templates are available on the CD-ROM in the back of your book)

(Answer to the photo of the shapes of dry land: *That photo from space is of the Sinai Peninsula in Egypt above the region of Mt. Sinai, where God gave the 10 commandments. Can you find it on your globe? The water you see is the Red Sea. Where do you think Moses crossed?)*

Reaching Out
to His World

It's a big world! Think of all the roads that meander through Europe, trek up the mountains of Asia, trail through the outback of Australia, wind across the savannahs of Africa and crisscross back and forth across North and South America! Then try to think of the 6 *BILLION* people who live on those roads! What did they eat for breakfast? What are they wearing? What language do they speak? What are all those people on all those roads doing right this very minute as you sit here reading these words?

You may not travel to all the continents in the world—and you never are going to meet *all* of the people who share our Earthly home with you.

What can you do to reach out to all of those people? You can pray for them! For the Bible says in 1 Timothy 2:1–3 that we are to pray—pray in every way we know how, for *everyone* we know! God asks us to!

Operation World is the name of an organization which can help you "know" everyone on our Earth home! Operation World will tell you more about the people living in every continent, every country of our world and what they need prayer for! You will learn what language they speak, what it is like to live where they live, and how you can best pray for them!

- Take ten minutes everyday to pray for the specific needs of the Earth's continents as posted here: http://www.24-7prayer.com/ow/ Don't let the Great Commission be your omission: **Go into all the world—every day—on your knees!** It will change your world. And the whole world.

- You can make Operation World's *Pray Today* website page automatically open on your computer's web browser. Simply click on the Tools function on your browser's toolbar, then on to "Internet options." Just type in: http://www.operationworld.org/today/ in the "Home Page" option. Then each and every time you open up your computer's web browser, information about a new country will appear on the screen so you'll know how to pray for the world!

- You can purchase Operation World's map of all the continents of the world and place it on a wall in your home. Soon you'll find yourself praying for the specific needs for the world's people. Check it out at: http://www.gmi.org/ow/index.html and click on "resources."

Further Explorations

Where on Earth? --- A Geografunny Guide to the Globe *by Paul Rosenthal*
(read independently Gr. 4-7, read aloud younger) With amusing cartoons and lively, tongue-in-cheek text, this guide to world geography makes the facts memorable! Anything but boring, this informative book cleverly tours middle grade students around the world so they learn first hand how "geography shapes lives, history, and traditions." Intelligent and entertaining!

Somewhere in the World Right Now *by Stacey Schuett*
(Gr. 1-4) It's one o'clock in the morning. Do you know what is happening on the other side of the world? Haven't you ever wondered? The world is a very alive, happening place! A captivating, poetic read, this story tours children around the planet to see exactly what is going on at the same time in other locales. What do the plains of Kenya look like in the early morning dawn? How do sun's first rays stream over India? Join a worker for lunch in Russia. Follow the action around the earth with the time-zone map on the end papers.

The Armadillo from Amarillo *by Lynne Cherry*
(Gr. 1-3) A curious Texan armadillo's rhymed-verse explorations lead readers on a map-skill adventure around the globe. Come ride on the back of a golden eagle, then board the space shuttle for an outer-space perspective of "where in the world are we?" An intriguing text which will lead into many other learning possibilities.

Around the World: Who's Been Here *by Lindsay Barrett George*
(Gr. 1-4) Join Miss Lewis on her nine month trip around the world! Read her letters to her science class of highlights of notable creatures she encounters on her adventures. In Kenya she sees evidence of "trees from which bark has been stripped" and queries, "Who's been here?" The next page reveals a beautiful painting of an African elephant and her calf. Follow Miss Lewis travels with the inset maps on each page and trail of her world tour on the endpapers. Go meet the wildlife God has created around the world!

How to Make an Apple Pie and See the World *by Marjorie Priceman*
(Gr. 1-3) Travel throughout Europe, Asia, South America and North America on this "world-wind" trip for the ingredients to make an apple pie! Then invite all the friends you have made from around the world! A beautifully fun geographical read while eating apple pie (recipe included)!

Hottest, Coldest, Highest, Deepest *by Steve Jenkins*
(Gr. 1-4) Go explore the heights and depths of God's world with these colorful illustrations from around the globe. Where is the world's highest mountain, hottest spot, wettest place? Creative charts help readers to place each location in perspective so that explorers can genuinely appreciate the wonder of each site! A perfect way to whet the curious appetite of young geographers!

Check out the series of books *by Michael and Jane Pelusey* entitled after each continent (Gr. 4-6) Explore each of the continents with this series of books by Michael and Jane Pelusey. Travel the varied climates, landscapes and people that make each continent so unique.

Too-Fun-to-Resist Excursion!

CRAZY CONTINENTS!

Have you ever laid on the grass, staring up at the clouds floating by, and tried to figure out what the shapes of the clouds looked like? Perhaps you saw big cowboys with flopping hats ride overhead in those white puffs.

Well, why don't you pull out your atlas and stare at the continents. What unique, interesting shapes do you see each continent making?

Materials needed:

~ atlas or globe
~ paper, pencil, pencil crayons
~ a creative imagination

Ready To Go? Let's Head Out!

~ Lay out your atlases and find a full page spread of all the continents on Earth. Can you find the wide-eyed Europa? The zebra of Africa? Does Australia look like a little cloud to you?

~ Trace the shapes of the continents onto your paper. Now draw in the features and details of the shape you saw. (For instance, if you think South America looks like an ice cream cone, color the traced shape of the continent to look like one!)

~ Write a sentence or two (or paragraph) that explains what all those crazy continental shapes are doing together on one page! Have fun! God definitely did when He was creating our continents! He stood back and declared, ***"It is good!"***

Too-Fun-to-Resist Excursion!

A GOOD N-E-W-S TREASURE HUNT!

Who can resist a good treasure hunt?! Isn't it always a thrill to find that which is lost!

If you follow the directions in this game carefully, not only will you find the treasure, but you'll never got lost again!

Materials:

~ a suitable snack treat (a box of raisins, fruit, a bag of nuts, wrapped goodie – whatever your preference)
~ a yard, park or large size room

~ an enthusiastic geographer or two!

Ready To Go? Let's Head Out!

~ Hide your snack treat in a location unbeknownst to your geographical treasure hunters.

~ Gather the geographers in a location some distance away from the hidden treat

~ Then call out directions for the geographers to walk: *"Head North! Turn West! Now South! Oh, don't bump into that—turn East! Now back South!"* Continue to call out the cardinal directions until your geographers discover their treat!

~ Ask your geographers if *they* can now hide a treat for another person? Can they call out the directions and successfully help their fellow treasure hunters find that treat?

If they can, that is good N-E-W-S!

THE SWIRLING SOUP IN MY FATHER'S HANDS

Chapter 5

Hold out your hand. Does your hand look like your Daddy's hands? My Dad was a farmer with big gnarled hands, weathered from his years of working in the fields. And no matter how my Dad scrubbed, his rugged hands were always creased with traces of grease from tractor engines. My Dad's hands smelled of work and the earth and I liked it. I thought those rough old hands could do just about anything.

Have you ever thought about what our Father God's hands must look like? His Word says that, He **"has measured the waters in the hollow of his hand"** (Isa. 40:12). Hands like that are truly beyond comprehension or understanding! How grand our heavenly Father's hands must be if *all* the waters of Earth could rest in one of his cupped hands! How much water of the seas *is* there on our Earth?!

Do you recall our imaginary walk through the layers of the atmosphere? Or how we puzzled over continental shapes of dry land? Now, from way off in your spacecraft out in the Universe, if you drew back those atmospheric curtains and looked down on our home of Earth, it wouldn't be the land that captured your gaze, but the striking blueness of our home. All that blue over all the Earth is *all* water!

Why, every one of us living on Earth actually lives on an island surrounded by seas of blue! An island is a mass of land surrounded by water. Everyone living everywhere on Earth is surrounded by water! If we divided our Earth into 4 equal parts, the dry land would cover only one part of the Earth, and water would completely cover the other 3 parts! The Bible tells us that,

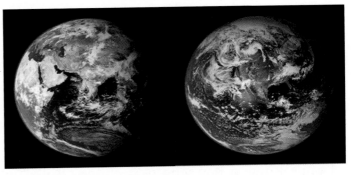

Water, water everywhere---almost! All that blue in our home is all water, which covers over 70% of the Earth's surface.

NASA

"God has founded [the Earth] upon the seas" (Ps. 24:2). God truly did establish our Earth upon the waters—326 million trillion gallons (1,260,000,000,000,000,000,000 liters) of water! (Check how many gallons your milk jug in the fridge holds—then picture trillions and trillions of those jugs filled with water!! Can you imagine?) Or think of it another way: If the Earth were an entirely smooth ball without any hills or valleys, there would be no land for anyone to stand on! For the whole of Earth, *everywhere*, would be covered in seawater 1 ½ miles (2.5 km.) deep. Not only can all of that water rest in the hollow of God's hand, but God, Himself, has measured out all that water! (Job 28:25).

The absolutely *only* place in the whole Universe that God made water was here on Earth! There is no place, *anywhere*, in the entire universe that you could stop your spacecraft and ask for a big glass of ice-cold water, except at our place—planet Earth!

Imagine your home having no taps for running water. No baths, no water to drink, no water to boil to cook food, no water for anything. So you took a pail and went outside to find water, somewhere, but there was no water outside—anywhere! Doesn't just *thinking* about living without water make your throat all dry and thirsty? Without water, none of us could live!

Does your Mom or Dad look like a big water bottle? Well, God made their body weight to be two-thirds water! We are made up of water! Neither could any of the plants or animals on Earth live without water! If you went out to your garden today, you'd find an earthworm—who is 80% made of water. God created the tomato you picked in the garden to be 95% water! And the birch tree in your backyard sucks up *twenty* 1-gallon jugs of water from the Earth on a warm day! Water is so important to us on Earth that more than *half* of *all* of us on this

"Mightier than the thunder of the great waters, mightier than the breakers of the sea— the LORD on high is mighty." ~Ps. 93:4

NOAA

planet live within a one hour drive of the sea! How we praise God for creating all that precious blue water we have on our Earth!

I once knew a boy who was called "Willy" when he was at home, "Billy" when he was at his grandparents' house, "William" when he was at church and "Will" when he was with his friends. He was called different names, depending on where he was, but he was just one boy! The Earth's ocean is much like that boy. Even though much of our planet is covered in water, there are not many oceans. There is really only one ocean on Earth. (No walls stop any ocean water from flowing to different parts of our Earth!) But we have named this one ocean five different names, depending on where the water lies.

If you pick up a globe, you may turn it such that at one time *all* you seem to see is Ocean! This water we call the "***Pacific Ocean.***" The Pacific Ocean is the biggest and deepest part of the world's ocean. When it is said that the Pacific Ocean is *big* that means 60 million square miles (156 million sq. km.) big! It would take 15 United States of Americas to fill up the Pacific Ocean! When it said that the Pacific Ocean is deep that means that in some places (like at the Mariana Trench) it is 6 *miles* (9.6 km) down to the very bottom!

Can you find the ocean shaped like a big fat "S"? These waters are called the "***Atlantic Ocean.***" Only half as big as the tremendous Pacific, the Atlantic Ocean is the world's most traveled ocean. Thus it is the Atlantic Ocean that has thousands of lighthouses dotting its shorelines, directing travelers safely through the waters towards home.

If you keep turning your globe, you will find the warm and stormy waters named the "***Indian Ocean.***" These temperate waters of the Indian Ocean are the only waters in the whole wide world that twice every year change the direction of their current, or the way the water flows!

At both ends of the globe, the North and South Pole, lie not sunny oceans but dark, freezing cold oceans. At the North Pole are the waters we call the "***Arctic Ocean.***" At the South Pole, lie the waters called the **"Southern Ocean."** The icy Arctic Ocean in the north is the smallest ocean of the world's waters. It also is the most mysterious ocean as one third of it remains ice that never melts. The frigid Southern Ocean around the Antarctica has the most blustery, strongest average winds found anywhere on the whole Earth. So navigating the waters of the Southern Ocean means to ride monstrous waves!

Those are the five names for just one magnificently diverse ocean!

Tell the folks at home all about it!

*What can you share about the water found on Earth? (**Memory Joggers**: Can you tell us something of how much water there is in the Earth's ocean? What makes our Earth different than any other place in the Universe? Can you name each of the 5 names of our globe's one ocean? Can you remember something interesting about each of them?)*

When I was sick, my mom would have me sip plain old chicken broth; no noodles, no colorful vegetables, just simple broth. Like that clear broth, you may think of the Earth's ocean, covering so much of our world, as a rather bland, lifeless area of our planet. For people can only live on the continents of this globe. Well, *people* may not be able to live in the ocean, but oh, the oceans are *swarming* with abundant life! Actually, there are more different kinds of life in the ocean than *anywhere else* on the entire planet!! Over 4,000 very different kinds of fish live in the warm Indian Ocean alone! From tiny, one-celled microbes to the world's largest creature, the tremendous blue whale, the ocean is sometimes called "a living soup," teeming with plant and animal life. God did not make the Earth's blue ocean like clear, chicken broth, but like the most colorful, lively soup you can possibly imagine!

Doesn't our ocean act like its living? Have you ever run teasingly along the seashore, the ocean water chasing after you, lapping at your heels? The Earth's ocean is never still, but always streaming, rising, falling, running. Like a restless child, our ocean is in constant motion.

One of the ways our ocean moves is in a streaming, flowing motion called a "***current.***" Currents are much like racing rivers. These "river" ocean currents flow in two ways: either near the surface of the ocean, or deep in the dark black of the oceans.

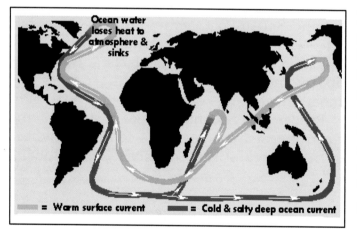

= Warm surface current   = Cold & salty deep ocean current

Warm water flows into the North Atlantic Ocean, cools, and becomes saltier because of evaporation. The water then sinks because it has become heavier. Then it flows south along the ocean floor to Antarctica, cools further, and flows out into the South Atlantic, Indian and Pacific Oceans. Here it warms, rises and flows back to the North Atlantic; the world's longest conveyor belt! *NOAA*

If you wrote a note to the folks at home, popped it into a bottle, and tossed it into one the world's largest surface ocean currents off the coast of Japan, called the Kuroshio Current, your bobbing bottle would be carried along at a speed of 75 miles per day! What creates such a rapid moving ocean current?

Wind mainly drives these surface ocean currents. Warm winds blow the Earth's ocean in one direction (west) and cold winds blow the ocean waters another direction (east)—so the wind forces our ocean currents to go around and around in circles! These circular currents are called "**gyres**." A **gyre** is a large, nearly circular, system of wind-driven currents on the ocean's surface. Ocean gyres in the Northern Hemisphere spin the same way as a clock spins, clockwise. (Remember that the Northern

60

Hemisphere is that part of the world that lies north of Earth's invisible middle line, the equator.) Ocean gyres in the Southern Hemisphere spin in the *opposite* direction, counterclockwise.

Why do some ocean gyres flow in one direction and other ocean gyres flow in another direction? The unique rotation of the gyres is a result of our rotating Earth. Geographers refer to this intriguing effect as the **"Coriolis effect."** Simply, the **Coriolis effect** is the tendency for moving objects, such as gyres, traveling large distances on the Earth's surface to actually bend, or veer, either to the left or to the right. Thus, the Coriolis effect is what causes water moving in wind-driven gyres to flow to the right in the Northern Hemisphere and to the left in the Southern Hemisphere. The shape of Earth's continents, the force of wind patterns, and the veering, bending Coriolis effect, are combined by God to form the massive surface currents of our globe's oceans.

In the black depths of the ocean are other currents, *deep* ocean currents. Surface currents or gyres are much like streams of warm water floating on top of the much colder, *deeper* currents. The deep ocean currents, running invisibly along the floor of the ocean, make up the longest river in the world! This deep invisible current weaves its way *all* around our globe! Do you recall the conveyor belt at the grocery checkout that moves your groceries along? These deep ocean currents create the longest conveyor belt you can imagine! (And the slowest!)

The deep ocean current conveyor belt begins in the North Atlantic where the water is frigidly cold. Because the water in the North Atlantic is so icy cold, it is heavier. What does something heavy in water always do? That's right! It sinks! So this cold water sinks to the black depths of the ocean floor and crawls along at a pace of no more than 14 ft (4.25 m) per hour. Slinking its way southward, right down to the South Pole, it then flows northward into the Indian and Pacific Oceans. All the while, the deep conveyor belt creeps so slowly that it may take hundreds of years for water from the North Atlantic to make its way to the Pacific Ocean down here in the dark deep river! When having finally arrived in the Pacific Ocean, the current warms. When the water warms, it rises up closer to the surface...and journeys back to the Atlantic to begin the cycle again! This conveyor belt does not bring groceries to the check out.

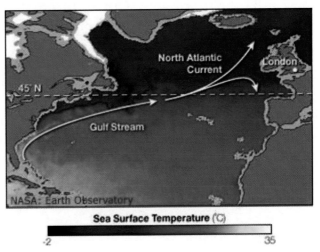

Sea Surface Temperature (C)
-2   35

The Gulf Stream, an ocean current that is 100 times larger than the sum total of all the rivers of the whole world, brings warm water—and weather—to places far north of the Equator!   *NOAA*

Instead it brings vast volumes of warm waters from the Pacific up to the chillier North Atlantic! Only God could create a massive conveyor belt like that!

God always does everything for a grand and glorious reason, doesn't He? So it is with ocean currents! Those ocean currents carrying warm water from the balmy areas of our globe to the colder parts of our world, bring with it warmer weather. Without such ocean currents bringing warmth, many people living in many places on Earth would be wearing heavy winter coats for months at a time instead of strolling about in light weight jackets.

One ocean current called the Gulf Stream brings such balmy water to Europe that over 60 million people live near its warmth. Do not think that because this ocean current is named the Gulf Stream that it is like a little rippling brook. The immense Gulf Stream moves 100 times as much water as *all* the rivers in the whole wide world put together! With the Gulf Stream hurrying along at 60 miles (97 km.) per day with all that warm water, (as you can see in this picture, showing the Atlantic's different water temperatures) far north of the Equator, in the country of England, palm trees can sometimes even grow!

The warm waters carried by the Gulf Stream changes weather to the extent that palm trees can grow far from the Equator! *NOAA*

Ocean currents also carry food to living creatures in the ocean, and then move those very creatures themselves along in its stream!

Currents carry not only food and warmth but also what fish and plants need to live: *oxygen*! That great conveyor belt takes oxygen from the air at the ocean's surface and, when those currents sink with heaviness near the cold North and South Poles, it carries down oxygen with it! So that deep-ocean conveyor belt *is* actually somewhat like the conveyor belt at your grocery store. It too brings to the ocean floor what plants and animals need to live: oxygen! If God had not created currents, the ocean floor would not be a teeming, living soup but a barren, lifeless place!

Tell the folks at home all about it!

*Tell me all you know about ocean currents. (**Memory Joggers**: What are "**currents**"? Can you explain what "**gyres**" are? What is the difference between surface currents and deep currents? What can you explain about deep ocean currents? Why did God create the ocean with currents?)*

We've explored one way the ocean moves: by currents. Yet there is another marvelous way that God moves the Earth's oceans!

The gravity of the moon, hundreds of thousands of miles away from Earth, tugs on the Earth's waters, creating tides. *NASA*

When I was a child, I used to sit beside my grandmother watching her sew, her pins holding bits of cloth together. When Grandma needed to pick up all of her pins, she would ask me to bring out a little magnet and *whoosh*! Invisible strings seemed to draw the pins all up to the magnet!

Did you know something very similar is happening to *all* of the water in the ocean? The moon exerts a strong, invisible force called "**gravity**" on the oceans, acting like a magnet, drawing Earth's waters towards it. **Gravity** is a force that causes one mass to be attracted to another mass. The bigger the object is, the more gravitational force it has to draw things unto itself. Even though the moon is 384,404 km. (239,000 miles) away from us, it draws the oceans to itself, much like that magnet pulled up my grandmother's pins!

See it in your mind like this:

← far side of Earth   * Center of Earth   close side of Earth -→   *Moon

Our Earth's ocean seems very far away when standing here on the moon. But the powerful pull of the moon's invisible strings of gravity stretches Earth's oceans out, pulling its water towards the moon, a bit like a pulled rubber elastic. Both ends of the elastic may have a bulge. The two bulging ends of the elastic are like the ocean waters of Earth closest and furthest away from the moon. This creates a wonder called "**high tide.**"

While you cannot see the invisible pull of the moon, you can see its result in the high tide! You may see high tide when you walk down the coast at one point in the day and see the boats bobbing high in the water at the dock. **High tide** is when the ocean waters rise high up on the beach or the coastline. Why, again, is the water high during high tide? Yes, because of the bulges created by the moon's pull on the Earth's oceans.

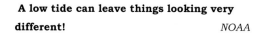

A low tide can leave things looking very different! *NOAA*

Now while you have bulges at the ends of your elastic, what does it look like in between the two bulges? It is low and stretched out. The oceans then on the sides of Earth in between the sides furthest and closest to the moon have a drop in water level, creating "*low tide.*" You may have experienced low tide when later on in the day, you head back down to the dock to go fishing on that bobbing boat, only to discover the boat beached in the mud and the fish far, FAR away out at sea! **Low tide** is when the ocean waters are at their lowest level on the beach or coastline. This boat found itself stranded on a sandbar as the tide receded!

Since the Earth spins entirely around once every 24 hours, there is a cycle of two high tides about every 24 hours: once when a location on the ocean is the closest to the moon, and once when it is the furthest away. Also, then, there must be two low tides every 24 hours, when that ocean location is in the two "in between" places.

As God created ocean currents, both surface and deep currents, for a grand purpose, so also did He create tides for wise reasons. Tides are much like giving the ocean's beaches and shorelines a cleaning, twice every day. People on our planet Earth can also produce electricity from the tremendous energy created by the rise and fall of tides. Only God could have created the magnificent dance of tides: all the rocking waters of the Earth rising and falling, carried along by an invisible attraction towards the encircling moon.

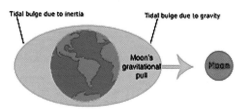

Looking at the diagram, can you explain in your own words how God creates tides? *NOAA*

Tell the folks at home all about it!

What have you discovered about Earth's tides? (**Memory Joggers**: *What is gravity? How does the moon's gravity affect the Earth's oceans? What is high tide? What is low tide? What creates tides? How often do tides occur?*)

The Earth's ocean is a *salty* living soup! In fact, if you drank the ocean's salty water, you might die! If the ocean is salty and we can't drink it, why did God create all that water?

God has created a process called "***evaporation***" that lifts the water from the ocean and forms it into clouds. (We will further explore evaporation in another adventure.) Do you know how MUCH water evaporates from the ocean to make clouds? About 92 quadrillion gallons (418 quadrillion liters) of water evaporate from the ocean every year to form rain clouds! When you gaze up at those feathery white clouds sailing over your head, remember the staggering volume of water that is drifting by! The average puffy cloud floating by actually weighs about 400 tons (362 tonnes) and contains about as much water as an Olympic size swimming pool!

Perhaps that is why God said for sky to appear, to separate the waters in the clouds *above* the Earth from the waters of the ocean *on* the Earth (Gen 1:6), because both our sky and our ocean are water, water, water! Geographers call this the "***hydrosphere.***" The word "***hydro***" comes from the Greek word for "*water.*" So the "water sphere" refers to all the water on the Earth or in the air around the Earth.

In the process of evaporating those millions and trillions of gallons of ocean water *on* Earth into clouds of water *above* our Earth, all the salt is left behind in the ocean! What falls from the clouds here on the continents where you and I live is FRESH water, completely free of salt! God has created a purification system for all the Earth's water, removing the salt from it so we can drink clean, fresh water! Don't you agree that when God made our Earthly home at creation, He really could say, "It is *good*!"

Think of it: All of Earth's ocean waters, teeming with life, flowing and streaming in surface and deep currents, rising and falling by the pull of the moon, all of the millions and trillions of gallons of water in Earth's one ocean with five names—all of it can rest in the hollow of Father's awesome hand.

Oh, don't you want to bow down and worship our Creator? Someday all of **"the earth will be filled with the knowledge of the glory of the Lord, as the waters cover the sea"** (Hab. 2:14).

POSTCARD HOME

What a day we have had, riding high on the ocean waves all around His glorious globe! Don't you want to write home and tell everyone about all this wonderful blue that He created for us on Earth!? Cut out your oversized piece of cardstock and draw a picture on the front of a hand holding all of Earth's oceans. Write the names of all of the oceans on the water resting in that hand! On the back, tell the folks at home a bit about the differences of Earth's one ocean with five names. Write about how the ocean moves—surface currents, deep currents and tides. Then give God the glory for the great things He has done.

(Postcard templates are available on the CD-ROM in the back of your book)

Reaching Out
to His World

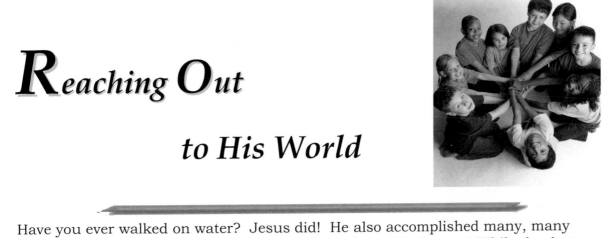

Have you ever walked on water? Jesus did! He also accomplished many, many other miracles, like making the lame to walk and the blind to see! While the doctors on the **Mercy Ships** don't walk on water, they do ride the waves of the ocean, bringing hope and healing to hurting people on our home we call Earth!

Mercy Ships is an organization of volunteers and doctors who sail the high seas of our world's ocean on hospital ships. Hospital ships are just that: hospitals that are on ships. These hospital ships sail into ports and welcome sick and needy people to come see a doctor and receive medical care.

Humphrey, from the African country of Ghana, was one of those people. Day after day, the children at school laughed at Humphrey because of his poor eyesight and crossed eyes. Humphrey often begged his mother to take him to a hospital to see if his eyes could be repaired. Then the Mercy Ships sailed south on the Atlantic Ocean and landed in at a port on the coast of Ghana. Humphrey traveled a long distance with his mother to speak with a doctor aboard the ship. A doctor decided that he would perform surgery on Humphrey's eyes. You should have seen Humphrey's smile when the bandages were removed after the surgery and he could see! Humphrey's mother exclaimed to the doctors, "God is here!"

Yes, God's healing touch and hope arrives for very grateful people like Humphrey when Mercy Ships sail the Ocean of our Earth.

What can you do to reach out and be a part of Mercy Ship's mission on the ocean waters? You could become a Mercy Shipmate and "sail" the oceans too! For a monthly donation of $25, you join with Mercy Ships to help children like Humphrey. You can sign up to be a Shipmate at: www.mercyships.org

But maybe you are thinking, "I am only young. How can I reach out to His world as a Mercy Ship sailor when I don't have $25 a month of help children like Humphrey?" Perhaps you could do what a girl named Deana whom I know once did. For Deana's first birthday, Deana's family asked guests not to bring a gift for Deana—but for Mercy Ships instead! Imagine how happy Deana and her family were to give enough money to Mercy Ships to pay for *seventeen* children, *just like her*, to have surgery to improve their lives!

Perhaps on your birthday you too might ask guests not to bring a gift for you, but a gift of money to send to Mercy Ships, the hospital that sails the world's Ocean! You too can become a "sailor" with Mercy Ships bringing God's healing miracles to ports all over our world! For more information about Mercy Ships, visit: http://www.mercyships.org/

Further Explorations

The Ocean Book *by Frank Sherwin*

(Creationist perspective) What lies beneath the surface of the world's oceans? This book, written with a Biblical worldview, will take you on an exploration the mysteries that lurk in the darkness thousands of feet below God's waters.

Roaring Waters *(Video) (Awesome Forces of God's Creation series--Moody)*

(Creationist Perspective) Hold on to your hat as you plunge down raging rivers, ride crashing tidal waves, escape surging floods and marvel at the ebb and flow of tides. Wonder at what water is, where it comes from and how God uses it to completely alter the landscape.

Waves, tides, and currents *by Daniel Rogers*

Learn about the different kinds of ocean waves, tides, and currents, how they are produced, and their impact on the climate and the world's shorelines.

Hello Ocean *by Pam Munoz Ryan*

(Gr. 1-4) Expressive rhymes, brilliant colors, and scientific fact orchestrate in this splendid book in a symphonic celebration of the ocean! Like a visit to the beach, one experiences the ocean with all five senses while accompanying the young girl of the text. "I see the ocean, gray, green blue, a chameleon always changing hue. . . . I hear the ocean, a lion's roar, crashing rumors toward the shore. . . . I touch the ocean and the surf gives chase, then wraps me in a wet embrace. . . . Sandy grains in a salty drink are best for fish and whales, I think." Revisit the wonder of the ocean again and again through the pages of this beautiful book.

Hotel Deep: Light Verse from Dark Water *by Kurt Cyrus*

(Gr. 3-5) Captivating artwork accompanies this text of 21 poems that explore the mystery of the ocean through the eyes of a lone sardine. "Where did everyone go?/One sardine. Apart. Alone./Welcome to the Mystery Zone." Danger and fear lurk throughout (and a reference to "a devil to pay" may want to be passed over.) A glossary of picture names some 28 marine species from the story. Exciting action, vibrant visuals, and fluid language make this a great-read aloud adventure of the underwater world.

In the Swim *by Douglas Florian*

(Gr. 2-6) Delightful, unforced playfulness weaves through these humorous poems about fish. A starfish, sporting sunglasses, declares, "And though it's true/I have no brain,/I'm still a star?/I can't complain." Full-page watercolor illustrations in muted tones couple each poem.

River in the ocean: the story of the Gulf Stream *by Alice Gilbreath*

(Gr. 5 and up) Learn more about the warm river flowing in the Atlantic Ocean and how it impacts our planet.

Awesome ocean science!: investigating the secrets of the underwater world *by Cindy A. Littlefield*

(Gr. 3-5) Dive into a hands-on introduction of the mysteries of the watery world. Go investigate general oceanic principles, waves and currents, shorelines and tide pools, the ocean floor, marine life, and ocean conservation.

Scholastic atlas of oceans *by Donna Vekteris*

(Gr. 4-7) This book offers a good overview of the workings of these marine ecosystems and explores some of the unique characteristics and features of the five oceans and the five major seas.

The seven seas: exploring the world ocean *by Linda Vieira*

(Gr. 2-5) Each of the fourteen double-page chapters in this book opens with a heading that begins with the phrase "The Sea Is." Along the way, learn more of the world's explorers, pirates, researchers, and a myriad of other intriguing material.

Too-Fun-to-Resist Excursion!

TUGGING TIDES!

Like a beautiful poem, the Earth's oceans chase the moon, rising to meet her. God has created such a lyrical dance of life here on Earth. Would you like to make your own tugging of the tides?

Materials:

~ the lid of a shoebox
~ tape
~ pencil
~ crayons

~ circle of white paper with a 5 inch (10 cm) circumference
~ rubber band
~ string
~ button or quarter

Ready To Go? Let's Head Out!

~ Cut your 5 in. (10 cm) circumference circle out of white paper. Can you color it to look like our Earthly home? Sketch in the continents and name those 5 oceans with one name. Having a globe or map in front of you will help.

~ Now push the pencil up through the shoebox lid, near one end. (The pencil should now be standing straight up, vertically.)

~ Tape (or glue) the circle of Earth about one inch (2 cm) in front of the vertical pencil, on the shoebox lid. Slip your rubber band around the pencil.

~ Now tie the center of your string around the middle of the rubber band. Leave two equal lengths of string at each end. Place your quarter or button on the shoebox lid at opposite end of the pencil. Think of this quarter or button as the moon.

~ Tape one end of the string to the center of the Earth circle. Tape the other string end to the moon quarter.

~ Slowly and gently tug on the moon quarter in a direction away from the pencil until the string attached to the rubber band is straight.

~ What shape is your tugged rubber band? Is your rubber band pulled into an oval shape, one pointed end towards the quarter moon, the other pointed end towards your pencil? How does your model show how the moon's gravity effect tides here on Earth? Why don't you show your model to someone and explain to them the wonder of tides!

And to think that all that water in Earth's one ocean is tugged by that far away moon!

Too-Fun-to-Resist Excursion!

ANYBODY SEEN MY SHOES?!

When I was young, I once accidentally dropped one of my shoes in a river. It was rather unnerving to watch my shoe lazily drift away on the current. But how about 60,000 shoes—on an *ocean* current? It happened! And has anybody seen those shoes?   Well, yes! What a story!

On a cold day in the spring of 1990, a freighter ship was chugging across the North Pacific Ocean when a violent storm whipped up. Tossing and falling upon the writhing sea, the ship finally lost 5 large containers from its deck, a monstrous wave stealing them off to sea. Slammed about on the hurling ocean, four of the containers split open—and sent 60,000 shoes out on the waters of the North Pacific Ocean. Where did those shoes go? Night and day, on stormy seas and quieter seas, the shoes were carried on the ocean currents...and one by one washed up on the shore. Can you find the places where these shoes washed up?

Materials:

~ map of North Pacific Ocean
~ pencil

Ready To Go? Let's Head Out!

(If you don't have experience with maps and finding positions of longitude and latitude, ask an older geographer to help you out. We'll explore the intriguing stories of longitude and latitude in an upcoming adventure!)

~ Find the following locations and number each one on your map:

1. May 27, 1990: 60,000 shoes into the sea at: 48 North, 161 West

(find the latitude of 48 North first – look for the country of Japan – then slide your finger over until you find 161 West – in the middle of the North Pacific Ocean—write a number 1 at this location)

2. 200 shoes recovered	49N 126W
3. 200 more shoes recovered	47N 125W
4. 100 shoes recovered	53N 131W
5. 250 shoes recovered	59N 139W
6. 150 shoes recovered	44N 124W
7. 200 shoes recovered	40N 124W
8. 200 shoes recovered	55N 130W
9. several shoes recovered	19N 155.5W
10. several more shoes found	32N 132 *EAST*
11. several shoes recovered	54N 133 W

Now can you connect all the dots? From the dots of where the shoes washed up, do you see the circular shape of a gyre?

And after those shoes floated along those ocean currents for all those days and nights, the shoes washed up on shores, people scrubbed off the sea wood and **wore** those shoes! The lost shoes had been found—swept home on an ocean current!

THE WOODSTOVE OUTSIDE THE WINDOW

Chapter 6

I know a woman who lives around her stove. There, in the center of her home, stands this iron-black, hulky woodstove. Daily she stokes the fire in this stove. That stove warms the quiet woman, and boils her water in the tea kettle, cooks her food, dries her clothes, and crackles away beside her as she rocks into the evening, with her knitting on her lap. That faithful woodstove is the center of the quiet woman's home life.

Did you know that all of us living in Earth's home revolve around our own woodstove? The massive, burning ball called the **sun** is like this planet's own woodstove! While the woman's woodstove burned wood to produce heat, the sun itself is not really burning anything but is powered by a very different process called nuclear fusion. Yet the sun and the woodstove are similar in that they both produce life-giving warmth. The sun is the center of our universe, and we revolve around its heat. While the woman lived close around *her* woodstove, the sun is about 93 million miles (150 million km.) away from our home! If we were any closer to our woodstove, we would burn up! While the quiet woman's fire may only get as hot as 500 F (260 C), the surface of the sun is 10,000 F (5, 540 C)—and the center of the sun is 25 million F (15 million C)! A hundred and nine times bigger than our Earth, the sun, made the perfect size at the perfect temperature, has been perfectly placed by God at just the perfect distance from Earth.

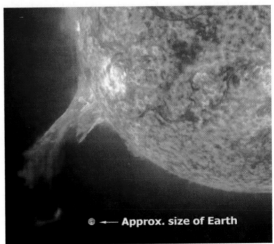

☉ ←— Approx. size of Earth

It would take 332,950 Earths to equal the weight of the sun! God perfectly placed our Earth the perfect distance from the woodstove of the sun! (Imagine if we were closer to that fireball of Sun!!)   *NASA*

Like the faithful woodstove that was necessary for living for the quiet woman, so the sun is necessary for life here on Earth. Why, did you know that it is the sun that gives Earth seasons and climate and weather!? Let's curl up together and explore how our Earth home lives around its own perfect woodstove.

As you read this page, what **season** are you experiencing where you live? There are only four seasons to choose from: winter, spring, summer, and autumn. What season you are living in all depends where on Earth you are living, and where the Earth is in its revolving, annual trip around its own "woodstove," the sun. For it is the sun, and the Earth's dance around it, that creates the seasons of winter, spring, summer and autumn that we experience on this planet.

Like a top, Earth spins around on its own axis. But do not suppose there is any great rod through the center of the Earth, for the axis of the Earth is an imaginary line.

Picture in your mind's eye a toasty warm woodstove in the center of your room. You are sitting near to it, playing with a spinning toy top. (Let's call it a spinner.) Envision that your spinner is decorated like a globe. Through your spinner is a steel rod. This is the **axis** on which your spinner rotates. An **axis** is a line around which an object turns. Think of the steel rod's handle as the North Pole and the pointed bottom of the rod (the part that spins on the floor) as the South Pole. The Earth too has an axis on which it rotates, just like your spinner!

Now if you twirl your spinner, you may notice that it tilts on a bit of an angle. The spinner's handle is not pointing straight up towards the ceiling at all, but it is tipped, pointing on an angle towards the peak of an evergreen tree, outside your room's window.

Earth is like that toy top! Earth spins on its axis with a permanent tilt. As Earth spins, it is tipped on a 23.5 degree angle. While the spinner's handle is tipped towards the peak of the evergreen tree outside the window, Earth too is tipped, towards the North Star, Polaris.

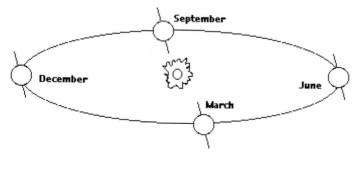

As the spinner begins to twirl on the east side of the stove, the sharpened point of the spinner is closer to the woodstove than the handle of the spinner, which is tilted away, pointing on an angle towards the evergreen tree peak. Thus, the bottom section of the spinner warms more as it most directly faces the stove. This is like the Southern Hemisphere of our Earth basking in *summer* because it is receiving

74

more direct sunlight from the sun while the entire Northern Hemisphere, tipped furthest away from the sun, is shivering in the cooler temperatures of *winter*. When the Earth is in this position in its revolution around the sun, it is called the **December Solstice**.

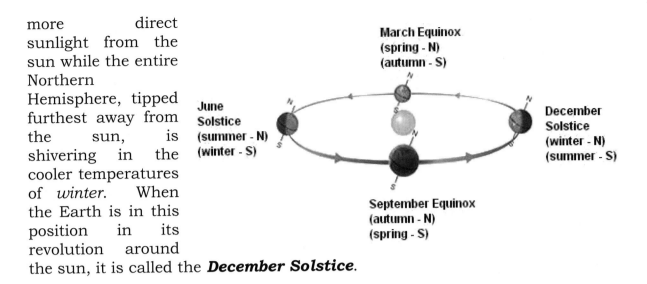

Now the spinner circles to the north of the stove, maintaining its tilt, the same angle, towards the evergreen peak. As the spinner revolves to the north of the woodstove, both the top and bottom halves of the spinner receive equal amounts of warmth from the woodstove. This is likened to the season of *spring* for the Northern Hemisphere and *autumn* for the Southern Hemisphere. This is a time when the Northern and Southern Hemispheres receive nearly the same amount of sunlight and is called the **March Equinox**.

Imagine our whirling spinner having now spun around another quarter turn around the stove, to the west of the crackling hot woodstove. Its handle is still tipped the same direction, pointing still towards that evergreen outside. Now that tilt toward the evergreen outside is also the tilt towards the toasty woodstove. This would result in the top half of the spinner receiving more direct warmth from the stove than the cooler bottom half. This is like *summer* in the Northern Hemisphere, when the Northern Hemisphere has its maximum tilt towards the sun, and *winter* in the Southern Hemisphere. When Earth is in this position in its revolution around the sun, it is called the **June Solstice**.

Then the spinner revolves to the south of the glowing woodstove. Again, both the top and bottom halves of the spinner are receiving equivalent amounts of direct warmth from the stove. What season is this likened to? Yes, this is *autumn* in the Northern Hemisphere and *spring* in the Southern Hemisphere. This is called the **September Equinox**.

Finally, the spinner orbits back round to the east side of the woodstove again, where it all began. Your spinner has just made one complete revolution around the woodstove, like the Earth makes one complete revolution around the sun—and you have grown one year older!

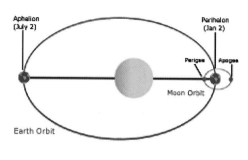

Earth's distance from the sun does not create the seasons, but rather the Earth's tilt and revolution creates seasons! *NOAA*

When I was young, I thought summer glowed down warm upon me because the Earth moved *closer* to the sun. I thought that when the Earth was *further* from the sun, I had to dig through the closet for my mittens. *Don't* think that! I was wrong! The changing distance between the Earth and the sun does *not* create the seasons at all! (Actually, the Earth is *closest* to the sun, a point called **perihelion,** around January 3rd—when I am building snowmen here in the Northern Hemisphere! The Earth is *furthest* away from the sun in its orbit, at a point called **aphelion,** around July 3rd—when I am swimming at the lake here in the Northern Hemisphere! So obviously, the distance of the Earth from the sun does **NOT** create our seasons!)

When I was a bit older, I thought that the Earth tilted one way to create summer, then changed its tilt to create winter. I pictured the Earth constantly tilting back and forth, back and forth, in different directions to create the seasons on Earth! *Don't* think that either! The Earth does *NOT* tilt back and forth to create seasons!

So, let's make sure that *your* thinking is right! The Earth is tilted on *one* angle that *NEVER, ever* changes: 23.5 degrees. No matter what time of year it is, the Earth's axis is *ALWAYS* tipped in the same direction, forever pointing towards the North Star. THIS tilt, and the Earth's revolution around the sun, is what creates seasons. The constant direction of the tilt means that for half the year the Northern Hemisphere is facing somewhat towards the sun, receiving more direct sunlight. And for the other half of the year it is directed somewhat away from the sun, receiving less direct sunlight. (The same holds true for the Southern Hemisphere.) It is *THIS* changing orientation of the hemispheres in relation to the sun that truly causes the seasons.

Is that not simply amazing? God placed the woodstove of the sun, at the perfect place in our universe, at the perfect temperature, and tipped our Earth the perfect angle, and sent our home revolving at just the perfect speed around the sun, all to create four beautiful seasons! It is just as God said, **" Let there be lights in the expanse of heavens...and let them be...for seasons**" (Gen. 1:14). God has promised that these seasons will continue to slip one into the other, year after beautiful year, as long as we live in this home, revolving around our woodstove: **"While the earth remains, seedtime and harvest, and cold and heat, and summer and winter...shall not cease"** (Gen. 8:22).

Tell the folks at home all about it!

Now that you have it all figured out correctly, tell us what you have learned about seasons here on Earth?
(**Memory Joggers**: *What angle is the axis of Earth tilted on? What direction does Earth's axis point? When is Earth closest and furthest away from the sun? Can you describe what position the Earth is in at December Solstice? March Equinox? June Solstice? September Equinox?)*

Although you may now understand how God creates the seasons of winter, spring, summer, and autumn here on Earth, you may be wondering why winter where you live means wearing a jacket as you bike down the street while winter for your cousin, living north of you, means wearing a snowsuit and building snow forts! Why are seasons experienced differently in different places on this planet? How you expect to experience the seasons—actually, how you expect to experience *every* day, all year long—is called **climate.** Climate is how the atmosphere outside your window "behaves" over long periods of time. Climate is how we come to expect our seasons, year in and year out, to act. What creates climate? What makes the atmosphere outside your window behave the way it does?

If you think again of that quiet woman living around her stove, you'll be on the right trail! It all comes back to the the sun that God created for our home!

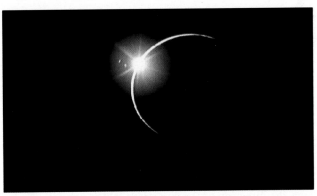

The farther north or south you live of the equator, the more slantingly the sun's rays fall upon you, therefore the cooler your days will be.   *NASA*

If you curled yourself up like a ball, your back facing the woodstove, the atmosphere around your waist, right at your belt line, would get very hot. That's because your waistline would be receiving direct heat waves from the woodstove. But your neck and your legs would not be as hot. That would be because the heat waves would be hitting them less directly.

The relationship between the sun and the Earth is somewhat similar. Since the Earth is a sphere, it too is curved, much like you stooped over next to the woodstove. From outer space you can actually see Earth's curve highlighted by the sun. The Earth also has a waistline—do you remember? Yes, the belt of the **equator** that wraps around its middle! The **equator** heats up more than any other area on Earth. The sun's hot rays hit the Earth's equator almost directly each and every day of Earth's 365-day, yearly revolution around the sun. (So it's *always* like summer at the equator!) The sun's rays hit the Earth *less* directly the further you travel north or south of the equator, so these places on Earth are less warm.

It is the distance you live from the Equator, and how directly the sun's heat rays hit where you live that causes the atmosphere to behave as it does. This is what makes **climate**. Remember that climate is the long-term pattern of the weather you experience every day.

The amount of heat that any part of our Earth home receives depends upon the direction of the sun's rays falling upon it. There are no real lines on Earth, of course, marking the different climates of heat and cold. But the plants and animals that live and grow on Earth do, in a very real sense, mark off divisions of climate. Certain animals and plants need a certain amount of warmth—or cold—to survive. And where they each live on Earth is a function of God's woodstove, the sun! By looking at this drawing, can you explain the angle the sun's rays that fall upon Earth in that region?

If, where you live, the sun's rays hit less directly for much of the year, your climate may allow you to go sledding and make snow forts nearly all year round. You live in a colder climate! (At the North and South Pole, which never receive the sun's rays directly, it is *always* like winter.)

If the sun's rays are streaming down more directly where you live, closer to the equator, your climate may allow you to make sandcastles at the beach anytime of the year. You live in a warmer climate! It all depends on where you live on the curved surface of the Earth and how directly the heat of God's woodstove, the sun, beams down upon you!

Tell the folks at home all about it!

I am so excited to hear what you have discovered about climate! (**Memory Joggers**: *What effects climate? How does the curve of the Earth and where you live on Earth affect how you experience climate? What is the equator?*)

Not only does God use the sun to create seasons, and long-term climate, He also uses the sun to create the **weather** we live in daily down here in the troposphere, even on a cloudy day when we can't even see the sun! Weather is what is outside your window, the conditions happening in the troposphere. And the sun is what drives it all.

To make weather, three ingredients are required: water, air and heat. Recall that God created 326 million trillion gallons (1,493 million trillion liters) of water that flow in our one ocean with 5 names. So our Earth certainly has water. We have explored the curtains of atmosphere that God created so magnificently for our home we call Earth. So our Earth certainly has air! And we have sat here today, warming ourselves by God's mind-boggling woodstove, the sun. So, yes, our Earth certainly has heat. Earth has the ingredients to make weather. So how did God design it? Well, it works much like the atmosphere in our room does.

Although you can't see it, our woodstove is stirring the air into circles in our room. The hot air is rising towards the ceiling. As soon as it gets away from the stove, rising up to the ceiling, it begins to cool off. As the air cools, it loses its lightness and falls back down towards the floor. At the floor, this now cool air will once again be heated by the woodstove and once more will rise.

The sun is doing the same thing in the atmosphere. The sun heats up the air, and, since warm air is lighter than cool air, the warm air rises, just like the hot air above our woodstove. Cool air, being heavier, rushes in to fill the space left by the warm air. This circular flow of air is called **convection.** Convection is the action of warm, less dense air rising and colder, denser air sinking. Convection creates "**wind.**" The word "*wind*" actually means to "*wind its way.*" Air generally winds its way around our globe in large circles called **convection cells**. Hot air rises above the Earth's "waist," the Equator, and cold air sweeps in from the Poles to take its place. From space, you can actually *see* where the invisible line of the equator lies on Earth by the line of clouds that

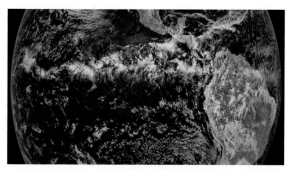

Can you draw your finger across the invisible Line of the Equator? Why can you "see" it from space?   *NASA*

gather overhead.   These clouds rise because of the intense heat from the sun hitting the "belt line" of Earth.

Like a circular chase around and around, the air rotates in our troposphere, making wind circles or convection cells.   Both the Northern and Southern Hemispheres have 3 separate cells of circulating winds: The **Hadley cell** of wind circles around Earth's belt at the equator. The **Ferrel cell** is the middle cell in each hemisphere.   And circling at the chilly North and South Poles are a **Polar cell**.

Tell the folks at home all about it!

What can you share with us about weather? (**Memory joggers**: *What ingredients are needed to make weather? What does the sun's heat cause air to do? What does air do when it cools? What is convection? What creates wind? What is a wind circulation cell? Can you describe how a wind cell behaves? What are the names of the three cells that circulate in each hemisphere?*)

While knitting and rocking next to the fire, the quiet woman I know often sets a kettle to boil on the woodstove, to make a cup of tea. What would I see soon, gently spouting up into the air of our room? Yes, the heat of the crackling woodstove would change the water in the kettle into steam or water vapor that would whistle across the room. Steam is actually just another form of water, water turned into a gas or **vapor**.   A similar process happens on our Earthly home.

The sun heats up the waters of the ocean. The heat of the sun draws some of these waters up into vapor. The process of the water turning into gas or vapor is called **evaporation.**   This water vapor is swooped away by the whistling wind.   As the air moves higher up into the atmosphere, the air cools down since temperatures are cooler higher up. Now, in the cool air, the water vapor **condenses** into water droplets. When you look out your window, you can see water vapor condensed into water droplets, for condensed water vapors are simply clouds! When the droplets become so big, and are too heavy to carry, the clouds release their baggage.   We experience that as rain, snow or hail, depending on the temperature and the types of clouds in the sky. This entire process is called the **water cycle**.

As the water of the ocean is always moving, so is the water above in the troposphere in constant activity. Water never stays in one place. Water is constantly evaporating from the ocean, lakes, or rivers, condensing in the atmosphere, falling again to the ground as precipitation (rain, snow or hail), then seeping slowly through our soil and out into a body of water, only to be evaporated again! A water vapor may stay up in a cloud for 10 days or a water droplet may remain circulating for hundreds of years in the bottom of the ocean. But all water is always moving. All water has always been and always will be part of the never-ending water cycle.

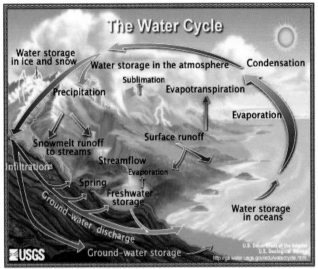

The ocean waters crash at your toes, but do you know how much water floats over your head? An average cloud holds enough water to equal the weight of 100 elephants! *USGS*

Did you know that the water that you and I drink, that runs out of your tap—all the water in the Pacific, Atlantic, India, Southern and Arctic Ocean—is the EXACT same water that God created on Day 2 of Creation? All the water that has ever been on Earth, at anytime in history, is the *very* same water that has been here since God made it at the beginning of time! In the clouds overhead may be a water droplet that Jonah and the great fish swam in! In your next glass of water may be one of the same droplets of water that Moses commanded to gush forth from the rock! For all the water there is now, is all the water there ever was!

That old woodstove drives life in the quiet woman's home. God's woodstove, the sun, drives life in our Earth home. For God uses the sun to give us seasons, climates and weather, everything outside our window! How we praise our God who **"changes the seasons"** (Daniel 2:21), who directs the sun across the skies to heat our world (Ps. 19:6) and who **"makes clouds ascend from the ends of the earth"** (Jer. 10:13)! Marvel at our God who **"loads the clouds with moisture"** (Job 37:11) and then **"brings the clouds...to water his earth and show His love"** (Job 37:13 NIV)! Oh, how we **"sing to God, extol[ling] Him who makes the clouds his chariot and walks upon the wings of the wind"**! (Ps. 68:4, 104:3).

Tell the folks at home all about it!

Put into your own words the cycle of water here on Earth.
*(**Memory Joggers**: Can you describe how a boiling teakettle is like our sun over the Earth's waters? What is a water vapor? Can you describe the process of evaporation? How are clouds formed?)*

POSTCARD HOME

Time to whip out your pencil and your oversized postcard and write a letter home about today's adventure around Earth's woodstove. On one side of your large postcard, draw a picture of Earth's spin around the sun. Draw the light beams from your sun in such a way that the folks at home can understand what creates our seasons. On the backside of your postcard, explain how God creates the seasons on our Earth. What causes some people to live in a warm climate while others live in a colder climate? How does God cook up the weather outside your window? How does the water cycle figure into the recipe? Can you sing His praises?

(Postcard templates are available on the CD-ROM in the back of your book)

Reaching Out to His World

Do you recall what the quiet woman did in the evenings as she rocked beside her woodstove? Yes, she often listened to the crackle of the fire while she knit away. Do you know how to knit?

Our Earth revolves and rotates around its own woodstove, which causes cool nights, frigid winter days and colder climates in parts of our world. And there are people, just like you and me, who need blankets to stay warm during chilly nights and hats and mittens in colder climates. Think for just a moment what it might feel like to experience the Earth's seasons or its cold winds without something like a blanket. How icy cold the floor would feel? How might a very drafty a blanket of newspapers feel?

What could you do to reach out to people in our world who need some warmth? Like the quiet woman, you could knit! Why not try to knit a blanket for someone who is feeling the cold, far from Earth's woodstove, the sun?

That is exactly what 25 children from New York, United States decided to do. They eagerly took up knitting needles and learned how to knit simple squares. As their teacher read aloud to them each morning, the children listened—and knit! When they had made 48 squares, they stitched all the knitted squares together—making a warm blanket for someone who was cold after losing their home in a disaster.

The children wanted to make more blankets....but they ran out of wool. So they wrote letters to yarn companies to donate yarn so they might keep knitting. And soon a big box arrived in the mail. The children squealed with delight as they unpacked skeins and skeins of colorful yarn. So the teacher keeps reading aloud...and the children keep knitting blankets!

You could too! While you listen to read alouds, you could be knitting up some warmth for someone who is not feeling the sun's warmth but a bitter wind whipping by!

To knit a simple square blanket:

Take one pair of 4.00 mm knitting needles and cast on 38 stitches. Now do a garter stitch for every row for 80 rows (18 cm). Then cast off. It's THAT simple!

56 squares will make one blanket for someone who is feeling the wind and the cold far away from Earth's own woodstove. Think of all the stories you can listen to while you knit God's love—and warmth—up for someone in need. Wherever you live, you'll be like the quiet woman, rocking and knitting beside your own woodstove, the sun!

(If you aren't sure where to find some yarn, check out your local thrift store. People often donate 1 or 2 balls of yarn. Or ask around to friends and neighbors.

For more information on how to make that knitted blanket, see:
http://www.cleckheaton.biz/news/Blanket_popup.htm

If you need more information regarding how to cast on or off, or do a garter stitch, it's as simple as following these easy instructions:
http://www.cleckheaton.biz/knitting_info.htm

And when you have completed your blanket, you can visit these charities to donate your blanket:

http://www.woolworks.org/charity.html

Your local Salvation Army location: http://www1.salvationarmy.org

Or the Mennonite Central Committee: www.mcc.org

Further Explorations

<u>The Seasons of Arnold's Apple Tree</u> *by Gail Gibbons*

(Gr. 1-4) In his apple tree, his secret place, Arnold invites young readers to discover seasons as he drinks in the fragrance of its pungent blossoms, bites into its sweet fruit, marvels at the gold of its autumn leaves.

<u>On the Same Day in March: a Tour of the World's Weather</u> *by Marilyn Singer*

(Gr. 1-6) Take a trip around the world in just a single day and experience a wonderful variety of weather! See first hand how geography effects weather! Hail falls in India, while sunlight "sparkles on the market in Senegal." Fog covers both a Louisiana bayou and the Nile River Valley. A delightful read stretching a child's weather consciousness.

<u>Down Comes the Rain</u> *by Franklyn Branley*

(Gr. 1-6) Join four exuberant children as they actively participate in a lively exploration of the water cycle. With text that invites reader participation, coupled with clear diagrams and engaging watercolors, this book creates a conversational atmosphere that sparks curiosity and learning!

<u>The Snowflake: A Water Cycle Story</u> *by Neil Waldman*

(Gr. 1-6) High up in the mountains in the month of January a snowflake falls. Melting, it flows into a river that feeds an irrigational system. Evaporating before falling as a drop of rain, the "snowflake" emerges from a set of taps and then travels to the ocean. Stunning art reinforces the wonder of the water cycle. The afterword suggests that the water we drink today may have once plunged over Niagara Falls or drifted in a jungle mist.

<u>The Cloud Book</u> *by Tomie De Paola*

(Gr. 1-4) Do you know the ten most common types of clouds? Or what clouds can tell us about coming weather changes? Dive into the pages of this classic author to learn more!

Oh Say Can You Say What's the Weather Today? *by Tish Rabe*

(Gr. 1-3) Travel with Dr. Seuss' cat in a hot air balloon and up through rain, snow, thunder, tornadoes and even powerful hurricanes! Your journey will also introduce you to thermometers, anemometers, wind vanes, cloud formation, humidity, fog and much more.

Sunshine makes the seasons *by Franklyn M. Branley*

You may feel the warmth of the sun and see its radiant light, but did you know how the sun makes the seasons experienced on our Earth? Discover how the only star in our solar system effects the life of everything living on our planet.

Water in oceans *by Isaac Nadeau*

(Gr. 4-7) Dive into the ocean and the water cycle and learn more of precipitation, solar radiation, evaporation and condensation. Accessible, scientific explanations are complemented by interesting illustrations.

Weather and the Bible *by Donald B. DeYoung*

(Creationist Perspective) A Biblically based book giving glory to God's power as seen in weather, the question and answer format explores such topics as tornadoes, acid rain, weather satellites, ball lightning and acid rain.

Weather *by Michael Oard*

(Creationist Perspective) With magnificent pictures of weather phenomena, this Christian author discusses climate zones, hurricanes, causes of various weather, and weather maps. Don't miss the fold-out spread in the back illustrating cloud types and storm development! You may also download a free study guide to this book at www.masterbooks.net.

Scholastic atlas of weather *by Donna Vekteris*

(Gr. 4-7) Two-page spreads look at the how, whys and wherefores of weather. Why not try the eight relatively easy experiments included?

Weather *by Seymour Simon*

(Gr. 3-6) How does the sun warm the Earth at different levels of intensity? How do wind patterns vary in the Northern and Southern Hemispheres? How do local climate changes fit into a larger perspective? Diagrams and stunning color photos introduce you to all this and more!

Too-Fun-to-Resist Excursion!

FEELING THE PRESSURE!

Do you ever feel like you are going around and around in circles? Air on our Earth really *is* going in circles! And that creates **pressure**. This is how it works:

Our air consists of molecules.   These molecules are constantly moving about in random motion, as if going in circles. The constant, random movement of these molecules is what causes **air pressure**. The more molecules within the air, and the faster those molecules are moving, result in greater air pressure. What changes air pressure? Air pressure changes as temperature changes, or if the amount of air changes as you go up in elevation.

Now if the temperature is warm, air rises, leaving behind an area of "*low pressure.*" Think of it this way: when something lifts off of you, you feel "*low pressure.*" So when warm air rises it creates low pressure. When air is cool, it is heavy, so it sinks. This makes an area of "*high pressure.*" You may remember it this way: when something heavy sinks down on you, you feel "*high pressure.*" So when cold air sinks, that creates high pressure.

With all of this air pushing and pressuring you, why don't you feel all the weight of that air directly over your head? That's because the pressure of air is applied equally to all things. For instance, if you held a sheet of paper out in your hand, the weight of air on that sheet would be over 1,300 lbs. But does the paper weigh that much? No! Because that same pressure (14.7 pounds per sq. inch) is also pressing up on the bottom side of the paper! So the air pressure applied *all* around us makes it such that we don't feel the actual weight of air!

But can you look around and *see* this changing pressure of air? Yes! What we need to see changing air pressure is a tool called a **barometer**. Let's make one so you can "see" how the air pressure changes in the next couple of days around your home! You'll be surprised at how easy it is to make a barometer to measure air pressure!

Materials:

~ a glass bottle (it must have a wide mouth as it is going to stand inverted)
~ a bowl

~ cardboard
~ water colored with food coloring
~ glue, pens, scissors
~ red pen, marker or pencil crayon

Ready To Go? Let's Head Out!

~ First fill your glass bottle with water. Then add several drop of your favorite color of food coloring (just so you can better see the effects. If you don't have any food coloring, you can just omit this step of the adventure!)

~ Place your empty bowl over the bottle and very carefully turn them both upside down, so that the bowl is sitting on the table and the bottle's mouth is on the bowl bottom. Before letting go of the bottle, make sure the bottle is standing securely on its neck in the bowl.

~ Now draw very small, equally spaced line divisions on the edge of your piece of cardboard (or cardstock), one right under the other. (It might be helpful to get out a ruler to draw the line divisions—mark a line division every two or three millimeters, or every tenth of an inch.) Glue or tape your cardboard onto the side of the bottle.

~ Take your red pen or marker (or pencil crayon) and draw a line on your piece of cardboard to mark the water level right now. Write today's date on the line.

~ Take your barometer outside very carefully (don't spill!) and put it in a shady spot. Check on your barometer each day. Has the water risen higher than the day before? Then the air pressure is higher! If the water level has fallen, the air pressure is lower!

How does the **barometer** work? When the air pressure outside is high, the air presses down on the water in the bowl. This causes the water level to rise in your bottle. So the higher the air pressure outside, the higher the water level in your bottle! Now you can *see* the pressure of the invisible air right outside your window!

Too-Fun-to-Resist Excursion!

THE WATER DANCE!

God has created so many circular dances on our Earth: circular, oceanic gyres, circular convection cells, even a circular water cycle.

Do you see the circle that Earth's water treads? The salt water of the ocean evaporates into the air, rises, condenses, forms clouds, gathers, and falls to Earth as fresh water, filters back through the soil to rivers, which run into the ocean...to begin this circular dance again! Would you like to make your own little water dance? (You'll have to partner with an **adult** geographer for this dance to ensure your own safety.)

Materials:

~ 4 tablespoons (60 ml) salt
~ 2 cups (455 ml) water
~ a pot on the stove

~ aluminum foil
~ a bowl

Ready To Go? Let's Head Out!

~ Let your adult geographer begin the dance by pouring the 2 cups (455 ml) of water into the pot and warming up the water on the stove. This is much like Earth's woodstove, the sun, heating up the waters of the ocean.

~ Now add your 4 tablespoons (60 ml) of salt. You wouldn't like to drink this water. It is much like the Earth's ocean water: salty.

~ Make a tent out of aluminum foil. Watch as your fellow adult geographer places the foil over the pot of water. Place a bowl as close as safely possible up along one side of your pot. Carefully allow one end of the foil to extend as much as possible over the bowl, while still being tented over your pot.

~ As your fellow geographer turns up the heat, watch the water come to a boil. The water in your pot is evaporating. Becoming vapor, the water is being carried up towards your foil tent. What is happening on the foil tent? Yes, it is condensing into water droplets, just like evaporated ocean water condenses into water droplets up in the clouds. Do you see your water slowly moving along the foil into the bowl?

~ Water should soon start dripping into your bowl.   What does it look like? When the water cools, dip your finger and then take a lick. What does it taste like? Where did the salt go? What has happened?

The same thing that happened on your stove top today, happens endlessly out at sea, especially at the equator. The woodstove sun heats up the ocean, the water evaporates, rises, condenses into clouds, and rain falls as fresh water, leaving the salt far behind in the ocean. Why don't you have a glass of water now...and marvel at the wonder of where all that water came from!

**"Who has measured the waters in the hollow of His hand,
And marked off the heavens by the span,
And calculated the dust of the Earth by the measure,
And weighed the mountains in a balance,
And the hills in a pair of scales?"**

Isaiah 40:12

GETTING TO THE CORE OF THE MATTER

Chapter 7

You know the rhyme—can you say it with me?

"Going on a Bear hunt!
Going to catch a big BIG one!
We're not scared. Uh Oh.
Can't go over it, can't go under it, can't go around it—
We'll have to go THROUGH it!"

Well, we aren't on a bear hunt, but on a discovery trek of our home, planet Earth! We know we CAN go over Earth. You walk over the Earth every day, everywhere you go. We certainly CAN go under the Earth. Just get on a plane and head around the Earth's sphere to whatever side of the world you want to call "under." (There really isn't an under to the rotating ball of Earth, is there?) And we CAN go around it. Sail a ship over the ocean waves, chug on a train across the continents, then hop on a super sonic jet when it is time for supper, and you will have traveled all around the entire circumference of Earth!

But we CANNOT go through Earth. We cannot send anyone, ever, down through the mysterious insides of our planet.

So our little rhyme for Earth would go like this:
"Going on a BIG trip,
Going to see BIG things!
We're not scared...
CAN go over it,
CAN go under it,
CAN go around it---but we CAN'T go through it!"

How do we actually know what is inside of Earth? No one has ever been there! After all, the deepest anyone has ever dug down into this planet is only about 7.5 miles (12 km.) deep. It took 20 years and over $100 million to dig that 7.5 mile (12 km.) deep hole in Asia! That immensely deep hole is like a mere **pinprick** compared to the 3, 975 miles (6,400 km.) down to the Earth's center!

As a child, I had an idea of what I imagined was at the core of the Earth, even if I never had been to the Earth's center. I thought the Earth had to be full of rocks—lots of them! I grew up on a farm and before my father could plant any seeds, we all had to pick the stones off the fields. No matter how many stones we picked, the next year there were always more. I figured that the Earth just kept gurgling up stones from deep within, like bubbles rising to the surface of a pond. But I wasn't sure because I had never been to the inside of Earth.

Earth is sort of like a big bag filled with a mysterious something. You can't peek inside the bag. You can't rip the bag open. You can't stick your hand into the bag. Which leaves you in a bit of a conundrum. How would you ever figure what was lurking inside your bag?

Maybe you would carefully monitor your bag to see if it ever *vibrated* or shook? Maybe you would watch for anything *blasting* out of the bag? Maybe you'd have some more ideas of what was inside if anything like steam or smoke ever *spewed* out of the bag?

Geographers face the same challenge. Geographers cannot peek into the center of the earth, open up the earth, or send someone down into the depths of the earth. So they do just what you would do!

Just like you monitoring your paper bag, geographers watch the earth for vibrating and shaking for clues as to what is inside earth. The Earth DOES shake and rumble! Such earth vibrations are called "***earthquakes.***" The sudden release of energy from an earthquake sends out different kinds of shaking movements throughout the planet. Geographers refer to these movements as "***seismic waves.***" (The word **seismic** comes from the Greek word for "*shaking.*" The earth is shaking like your bag might be shaking!)

Have you ever tossed a big rock into a pool of water? What do you see in the water? You may notice ripples moving outward in circles on the surface of the water. An earthquake is like a giant stone when thrown into a pond; it sends out seismic waves in all directions throughout the entire sphere of the Earth.

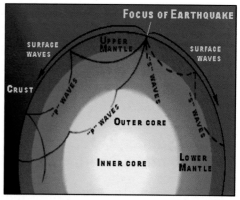

Geographers watch this shaking, these seismic waves, from over 3,000 seismographic stations all around the world. Like you'd record each little rustle of your bag, geographers record the waves of the approximately 8,000 earthquakes that happen EVERY DAY on Earth! (Most of us living on this planet don't even feel these rumbles and shakings, do we?!)

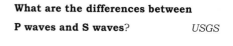

What are the differences between P waves and S waves?   *USGS*

As geographers measure the speed and direction of these seismic waves, they have discovered clues of what is inside this globe!   Earthquakes create two different types of seismic waves.

One kind of wave is called a **P wave** (Primary, or Pressure waves). The P waves are simply sound waves that travel through the Earth. The fast moving seismic P waves move just like your slinky toy slinks up and down. (Can you move your hand up and down like a slinky?) P waves, sound waves, can travel through both liquids *and* solids.

The other kind of wave created by an earthquake is called an **S wave** (Secondary, or Shear waves). Picture yourself playing jump rope with a friend. When you shake your end of the rope from side to side, doesn't the rope shake back and forth like a wriggling snake? S waves move back and forth, in a sideways motion, just like that snake-like jump rope. (Now try to move your hand like the snake-like S wave). S waves cannot travel through liquid. S waves from earthquakes can only travel through solid material. If an S wave bumps into a liquid inside of the Earth, it either bounces back, or turns into the slinky-like P wave.

Imagine an earthquake rocking and rumbling a country in South America. A geographer on the opposite side of the world in Asia might see P waves appear on her wave detector called a **seismograph**.   She does *not*, however, observe any S waves. "Aha!" she says (in her Asian language, of course). "There must be a layer of liquid inside the Earth between me and South America through which the S waves cannot travel!"   Just like this, geographers study the records of seismic waves of thousands and thousands of earthquakes. How these seismic waves behave give hints to geographers of the types of materials inside the earth: liquid and solid.

Tell the folks at home all about it!

*What do you know about seismic waves? (**Memory Joggers**: What kind of energy does an earthquake make? What does the word "**seismic**" mean? What are the 2 different kinds of seismic waves that earthquakes create? What is the difference between these two kinds of waves? Can you show the motion of the 2 waves with your hands? What happens when an S wave bumps into liquid in the earth's interior?)*

What if you saw smoke seeping from your brown paper bag? Or something actually *explode* out of the bag?!! If you closely examined whatever shot out of the bag, wouldn't you know more about the bag's contents?

Geographers monitoring Earth find that things actually shoot out from the inside of our globe! This extraordinary occurrence is called a "**volcano.**" A volcano is much like a mountain-sized chimney where material from the inside of the Earth spew out. (We will further explore volcanoes and earthquakes in another geographical excursion.)   Rocks from 60-95 miles (100-150 km.) deep in the interior of Earth are forced to the planet's surface in the explosions of volcanoes!   Geographers study these rocks to understand more of what is inside the Earth.

Now you might take all the information you have gathered about the shakes coming from the inside of your bag, about the material that blasted out of your bag and combine that knowledge with your understanding of how materials respond in various conditions, and you might still not know for *sure* what was in your bag. But you'd have some pretty good assumptions. Geographers have done just what you would do. While they are not positive as to what is inside of the Earth, they do have some theories.

Tell the folks at home all about it!

Can you share how geographers have come up their ideas of what is inside of the Earth? (**Memory Joggers**: *What have they learned from earthquakes? How do volcanoes provide clues to the make-up of the Earth's interior?*)

Do you remember how we went on our imaginary tour of the Earth's atmosphere? Why don't you get geared up and we'll embark on another imaginary tour. But this time, instead of heading up, up, UP, let's head down, down, DOWN! Down into what geographers *think* make up the inside of our Earth.

Did you bring an egg with you? Well, bizarre as it seems, we'll need to take a hard-boiled egg with us to really understand where we are going! (Not that the hard-boiled egg is a map, but it *will* give us some clues to where we are going!) With your hard-boiled egg in hand, soon you will see it as a picture of our Earth home?

The shell is what geographers refer to as the **crust** of the Earth. The earth's crust includes all of the world's land surfaces and the ocean floor. Did you ever think that you were walking around on a crust? Look at the shell of your egg. Isn't it very, VERY thin in comparison to the rest of your hard-boiled egg? The rocky crust of the Earth is just as thin in comparison to the rest of our planet. The crust is only 3 miles (5 km.) under the oceans and up to 45 miles (70 km.) thick under some continental mountain ranges. If we hopped in our car, it may only take us about half an hour (88 kph.) to drive down through the parts of the Earth's crust under the continents.

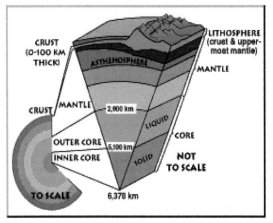

This is an artist's conception of what the interior of Earth may look like; a slice of Earth. Can you name the layers?   *USGS*

What is the Earth's thin crust made of?
While the crust of your grandmother's apple pie is all the same flaky pastry, the earth's crust is rather like ordering a pizza because there are two kinds of crust: thin crust and a thinner crust. The Earth's thin crust under the continents is made mostly of a rock called **granite**. But the Earth's even thinner crust under the ocean is composed of a dense, heavy rock called **basalt**. Together, these rocks form Earth's crust.

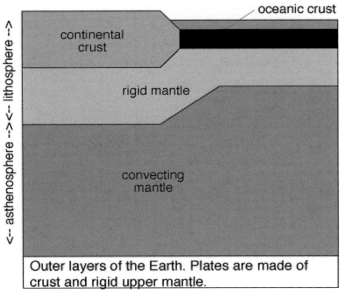

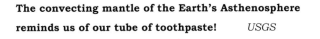

Outer layers of the Earth. Plates are made of crust and rigid upper mantle.

The convecting mantle of the Earth's Asthenosphere reminds us of our tube of toothpaste!   *USGS*

Now that we are through the crust, let's dig into the pie! Oh, but seeing as we left the pie at home and only brought the hard-boiled egg with us, we'll just have to dig into our egg! Can you cut your egg open? Do you see the different layers of your egg? We are leaving behind the shell of the egg, the Earth's very thin crust, and are now heading into the white of the egg, called the Earth's **mantle**.

The upper, solid layer of the mantle and the Earth's crust are together called the **lithosphere**. "*Litho*" comes from the Greek word "*rocky*," so lithosphere means the rocky part of our Earth, both the Earth's solid crust and the upper rigid portion of the mantle.

Much like the white of the egg is thicker than its shell, the mantle is thought to be much thicker than the Earth's crust, about 1,800 miles (2,900 km.) thick. That's 29 hours of driving in our car! (How many times would you haved asked "Are we there yet??!" in those 29 hours of non-stop driving?!) But the scenery of the Earth's mantle certainly would not be boring! The mantle, composed of various elements such as silicon, oxygen, iron and magnesium, is a place of change!

A few miles (km.) into our mantle exploration, we would be driving through a liquid even though it is a solid. The mantle is said to have "plastic behavior." Wouldn't it seem strange to gaze out the window at a solid material that can flow like a liquid? Maybe that is not as strange as you think!

Actually, you use a similarly strange material every morning when you wake up! When you wake up, do you stumble into the bathroom and grab a tube of toothpaste, then squeeze? What comes out on your toothbrush? Is the toothpaste a liquid or a solid? Or is toothpaste both? Well, parts of the Earth's mantle are just like your toothpaste: a flowing solid!

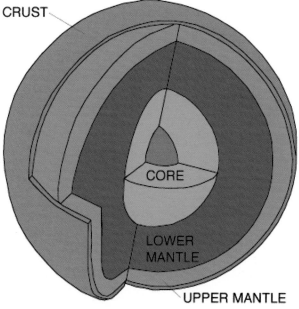

This region of the upper mantle is referred to as the "**asthenosphere.**" "Astheno" comes from the Greek word meaning "without strength," so the asthenosphere is the part of the mantle that is a weak, mushy, toothpaste-like "rock."

In other parts of the mantle we would be driving through some extremely dense, heavy rocks, much, MUCH denser than the rocks I picked off my Dad's fields. These rocks would be very dark in color because of their high iron and magnesium content.

Imagine marveling at the extraordinary scenery of the Earth's mantle: the soft and nearly liquid state of the rocks, while other scenery would be through areas of near brittle solidity.

But let's make sure we keep the air conditioner set on high to cool us down. The Earth's mantle is thought to be a steamy 2,880 F (1,582 C)! (Remember, you want to go swimming on a day when it is 85F (29C)—and the Earth's mantle is over 33 times hotter than such a hot day!) Actually, for every mile you would drive deeper into the Earth, it gets about 75F hotter! (25C/km).

Tell the folks at home all about it!

Tell me about the Earth's crust. (**Memory Joggers**: *What is it made out of and how thick is it? What is the layer under the Earth's crust? How thick is the mantle and what is it made of? What else can you remember about the mantle?*)

Are we there, at the centre of the Earth, yet? Not quite, but we are getting closer! If you look at your hard-boiled egg, we are now waving goodbye to the white of the egg, the Earth's mantle, and venturing into the egg's yolk, the Earth's **core**. The Earth's core is believed to be divided into the **outer** and **inner core**. Different than the yolk of your egg, the Earth's **outer core** is thought to be in a liquid, fluid state. Think of it as the liquid ocean surrounding the inner core. It is NOT, however, an ocean of water.

Have you got a nickel jangling around in your pocket? The Earth's outer core is thought to be made of mostly nickel and iron. While I suppose the nickel in your nickel is rather solid, the nickel of the outer core's ocean is rather runny—and scorching hot!

The Earth's outer core is thought to be about 1,366 miles (2,200 km.) thick, so are you ready for the 22 hour long trip through the Earth's waving, swirling, outer core? Turn up the air conditioning again and get comfortable! We may now be a long, LONG ways away from my front door......but whenever I'm lost and can't even find my front door, the Earth's outer core points me in the right direction!

See, the Earth's magnetic field comes from this deep ocean of iron-nickel. The liquid outer core of the Earth seethes and rolls like water in a pan on a hot stove. The churning of the liquid iron-nickel in the outer core causes charges to move around, which creates a giant electromagnet. So whenever I pull out my compass, and the magnetic needle points towards north, I have just used the magnetic field of the Earth's outer core! Think of all the lost people who have found their way home across oceans and mountains because God created the iron-nickel of Earth's outer core!

Tell the folks at home all about it!

*Describe the Earth's outer core. (**Memory Joggers**: What is the Earth's core made of and what is its state? Do you remember how thick the outer core is? What does the outer core create? Can you explain why God may have created this electromagnetic field in the Earth's outer core?)*

Well, can you take the unbearable heat and head into the inner core, the very center, of the Earth, about 6,370 km (3,960 miles) from your front door? While our hard-boiled egg gives the impression that there is simply one core within, remember that the Earth has a *liquid* <u>outer</u> core and a *solid* <u>inner</u> core.

The **inner core** of Earth is a solid ball of iron inside the ball of our Earth. Why is the inner core *solid* while the outer core is *liquid*? It is NOT because the inner core is cooler than the outer core. The inner core is actually hotter! In fact, the inner core is thought to be even HOTTER than the very surface of the sun—about 5,200K (or 9,000F)! But even in that mind-boggling heat, the inner core doesn't melt! Can you figure out why?

If you had more than a million pounds pressure on every square inch of you— the weight of the *whole rocky world* squishing down upon you—it would cause you to become frozen solid! Which is exactly the case for the Earth's inner core. Even though the temperature is so searing high in the Earth's inner core, the inner core is solid iron and nickel because of the intense pressure it is under.

The solid inner core of the Earth rotates and spins around just like the surface of the Earth. The inner core, however, is not attached to the mantle of the earth. (Remember, it is separated from the Earth's mantle by the iron-nickel ocean of the outer core.) Like its own planet within the planet of Earth, the inner core rotates. Yet it does *not* rotate at the same speed as Earth!

If you could roll down your window as we drive through the inner core, and if you could look up, way, WAY up, at the bottoms of the continents, (if you could see through all that rock!) do you know what geographers think you would see? You would see the continents falling behind you at a rate of a half-mile (.8 km) per day! In approximately 120 years, the inner core, like a planet within the Earth, completes one more extra turn around than we do on Earth's surface.

Are you ready to escape this blistering heat and head back home? Look at your hard-boiled egg to see our trip home in fast motion! Up through the scorching-hot solid inner core (spinning faster than we are at the Earth's surface), through the liquid ocean of iron-nickel of the outer core, through the variable mantle with its rockiness and flowing solids, up through the Earth's very thin, brittle crust—and ahhhhh, cool, fresh air again!

Do you remember how we said that the inside of Earth is like something hidden in a brown paper bag? Geographers aren't positive what is *really* inside of the Earth, but we have had a trip through what geographers *think* to be inside of Earth. Who knows for SURE what the Earth is made of? Why, the One who *made* our incredible home! While we could only embark on an imaginary journey through Earth, our Lord has *seen* the very inside of this planet. "**And the Spirit of God moved on the face of the deep**" (Gen. 1:2 KJV). God is the only One who knows EXACTLY what is deep within our glorious globe!

Tell the folks at home all about it!

*Tell us about your discoveries about the inner core! (**Memory Joggers**: How far have you traveled from your home to the inner core of the Earth? What is the difference between the inner core and the outer core of Earth? Why is the inner core not a liquid?)*

POSTCARD HOME

While you are cooling off, why don't you see if you can share the highlights of our deep Earth trip? What was the first layer we drove through? How deep is it? What is the earth's first layer made of? Then where did we drive through? What was the scenery out your window? Do you remember where we drove through the third segment of our trip? (Maybe your hard-boiled egg can give you a hint!) Why is this layer such a gift from God to people on Earth? And finally, what did we discover at the center of the Earth? What were some unique features of the center of the Earth?

Draw a picture on your postcard of what geographers think is inside of Earth, label the layers--- then write a summary of your wild adventures on the back! Add that postcard to your ring!

(Postcard templates are available on the CD-ROM in the back of your book)

Reaching Out
to His World

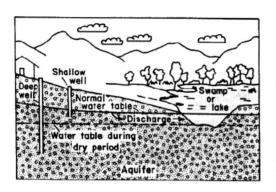

Digging down into Earth leads us to...
WATER!   *USGS*

If you picked up a shovel, rolled up your sleeves and started digging through the crust of our Earth, what might you find? It depends where you started digging. If you were at the beach, your hole might very quickly fill up with...water. What if you dug deep down into the Earth's crust...with a drill? Is your Dad six feet tall? Well, what if you drilled down into the Earth's crust to make a hole where 166 men, each as tall as your Dad, could all stand one on top of each other's head—1000 ft deep hole? Your drill has chewed through rocks and screwed itself all the way down in the blackness to find...water. For the water that falls from the sky, filters down through our soil until it reaches a layer of rock it can't flow through. This is called **ground water**, and forms the **water table**.

Now imagine digging the deepest hole in the world. (Remember, that the *deepest* hole we have dug is not even very far through the whole of Earth's crust—and the Earth's crust is the very *thinnest* part of the Earth's structure! So even though our deep hole seems very deep, it isn't very deep at all.) In the cold of the Arctic, on the Kola Peninsula, for nearly 25 years, scientists have been drilling through the Earth's crust and they thought they knew what was down there—but they were surprised! (Scientists often make assumptions about how the Earth is made that later prove to be incorrect.) Did you know that at depths of 7.5 miles (12 km) down into Earth's crust, scientists found...water? It was *not* ground water from rain or snow that had filtered down that far through the rocks. The water the scientists discovered had actually been a part of the rock itself, but had been forced out of the rocks by the sheer weight of the world pressing down upon it. Nonetheless, where scientists thought there would be solid rock, free flowing water was found! In the deepest hole in the world!

There is clean flowing water under our feet, in the Earth's crust, wherever we walk. Sometimes we just have to dig very deep to find it.

Count to 8.   During the time you counted to 8, a child just like you died because of a disease they contracted from the water they drank. And another one will die in the next 8 seconds. All the while, there is clean, fresh water down there in the Earth's crust, right below their feet. They just can't get to it.

Young people like 12-year-old Napoga from the African country of Ghana, need the clean water a well could provide. Napoga rises out of bed each morning at 5:30 to collect water for her family. And it takes Napoga at least 6 hours every day to collect that water because she has to sit and wait for the water to seep up through the ground. Then, when Napoga finally scoops it up in her gourd, the water is not clean like the water from your tap. Napoga's water is dirty and muddy—and it is the same water that the animals gather around to drink.

What can you do to reach out to people on this Earth who need the water that flows through the Earth's crust? Why not help a girl like Napoga drink fresh, clean water from down in the Earth?

Put a jar beside your sink. And every day, drop your pennies, dimes and nickels into that jar. When you turn on the tap for a glass of water, and see that change jar beside the sink, you'll be reminded how blessed you are to drink clean water, pumped up from down in the Earth's interior. And you will be collecting money to give someone like Napoga the same privilege!

(When your sink change jar is full, you can donate it to the following ministries that dig wells in countries all around the world to provide clean drinking water to families:

Operation Blessing: Living Waters Project:
http://www.ob.org/programs/living_water/index.asp

World Vision—see their Gift Catalogue and select Clean water:

http://www.worldvision.org

Partners International—see their gift catalogue Harvest of Hope, and give the gift of clean water http://www.partnersintl.org/welcome/)

Further Explorations

The Geology Book *by Dr. John Morris*

(Gr. 3-12) (Creationist perspective) Tour the earth's crust with Dr. John Morris. Discover the natural beauty and the scientific evidences of God's creation. A beautifully illustrated book; study earth's natural history from a creationist perspective. You can download a free study guide for this book at www.masterbooks.net.

The Magic School Bus Inside the Earth *by Joanna Cole*

(Gr. 2-5) Hop on a special school bus with Ms. Frizzle's class, and take a field trip through earth's interior. Learn at first hand what geographers theorize about different kinds of rocks and the formation of the earth. Keep your eyes open! Surprises abound through each strata down to the very inner core where it is hot, hot, hot. You'll collect rock samples with Ms. Frizzle's class before being expelled from the earth's core in a volcanic eruption!

How to Dig a Hole to the Other Side of the World *by Faith McNulty*

Join an imaginary 8,000 mile journey through the earth and memorably learn the earth's composition including topsoil, granite, basalt, steam, magma and mantle. With a whimsical bend for adventure, and explosively colorful illustrations, this book creatively explores the earth's geology!

Structure: exploring earth's interior *by Roy A. Gallant*

(Gr. 5- 8) (old earth/non-Creationist perspective) An informative description of the formation of the earth and the composition of its surface and interior. Watch out for the earthquakes and volcanoes!

Too-Fun-to-Resist Excursion!

TASTE AND SEE THAT THE LORD IS GOOD!

I'll bet you are ready for something cool and refreshing after that scorching hot trip through Earth! Why not make this refreshing Edible Earth!

Materials:

~ ½ gallon (2L) lime sherbet
~ ½ gallon (2L) chocolate ice cream
~ ½ gallon (2L) vanilla ice cream
~ ½ gallon (2L) strawberry ice cream

~ Chocolate chips
~ Large glass bowl
~ Plastic wrap
~ Hungry explorers!

Ready To Go? Let's Head Out!

~ So that your edible earth slides easily out of its mold, line your bowl with plastic wrap

~ Let the lime sherbet sit at room temperature until it is slightly soft. Now mold it to the bottom and sides of your plastic-lined bowl. You've just formed the **crust** layer of your Edible Earth! Return the bowl with the crust layer to the freezer for at least an hour before adding the next layer. (Do you remember which layer lies under the crust?)

~ Give your chocolate ice cream time to slightly soften. Mix your chocolate chips into the ice cream. (The chocolate chips will represent rocks.) Now mold a layer of chocolate ice cream on top of the hardened crust layer of lime sherbet. What layer have you just formed? Yes, the mantle! Again, return the bowl to the freezer for an hour. (But remember, the true mantle of Earth's interior would NEVER be cold! Do you remember the temperature of the mantle?)

~ Now, after your vanilla ice cream has softened, press it to the sides and bottom of your bowl. You have just formed the outer core! What can you recall of Earth's outer core?

~ Finally add the strawberry ice cream to the very middle. Yes, that represents the inner core! Why do you think strawberry ice cream would be a good choice to represent the inner core? What is the difference between the inner and outer core of the Earth?

~ You have formed all the layers of the Earth's crust, right to the scorching hot inner core! So you had better just cool off and freeze the mixture overnight. Keep it frozen until you are ready to serve.

~ Then **"taste and see that the Lord is good**!" Praise Him for the wonder of our home of Earth! While you eat, can you share with one of your guests the marvels of your trip through Earth and the different layers within Earth?

Too-Fun-to-Resist Excursion!

NAME THAT ROCK!

Earth's crust is made of rocks. You can simply go outside, pick up part of Earth's crust, tuck the rocks in your pockets to take home and examine. What do you know about rocks? You walk over Earth's crust and its rocks all day long. Maybe it is time to figure out what their names are, what they are made of, how they are different.

Can you say with the Psalmist David, **"The Lord is my rock, my fortress and my deliver"** (Ps. 18:2)? Maybe learning more about rocks will lead you to discover more about the character of God and why He is called our Rock!

Materials:

~ a thorough rock identification book from the library
~ magnifying glass

Ready To Go? Let's Head Out!

~ Look for rocks. They are everywhere! Gardens, new subdivisions where houses are being built, farmers' fields, river banks—start looking for rocks! Collect interesting ones, shiny ones, colorful ones. This is a wonderful way to spend an afternoon!

~ When you have spent some time looking for rocks and you are pleased with your specimens, begin classifying them. What colors are the same? Sort rocks together with similar texture.

~ Now spend some time identifying your rocks. Open up your library books and do some researching! Learn the different characteristics of rocks and what various categories rocks may fall into. Which category does each of your rocks fall into? Igneous? Sedimentary? Metamorphic? Cultivate your research skills and determine the differences between these categories. Label each of your rocks appropriately. Think of all you are going to learn!

Take some time over the next few weeks to really get to know your rocks. See how drastically our Earth changed because of the Flood! (Highly recommended reading: ***The Geology Book***, John Morris, Master Books.) After all your studying of the rocks of Earth's crust, do you know why our God is called our Rock? (Ps. 62:2)

SINGING, DANCING AND PRAISING GOD

Chapter 8

(Psst: Before you get curled up on the couch together, you'll need a hard boiled egg again!)

As a young person, I once nervously lined up on a wooden dance floor for an old-fashioned, country square dance. A man decked out in a brown cowboy hat called out how we were to move our feet. All of the square dancers' feet (except mine) dutifully stomped and clamped out the caller's rhythmical directions (my feet sort of stumbled through the directions!):

Heads Pass the Ocean, Recycle,
Pass Thru, Right & Left Thru,
DoSaDo, Make a Wave, Explode the Wave,
Swing Corner & Promenade...

The names of the directions for how to move our feet sound sort of funny, don't they? The square dancers, however, knew what each phrase like "*dosado*" and "*recycle*" meant. They skillfully moved their feet and hands in the way that is called "*pass the ocean*" and "*make a wave*".....

Did you know that the ocean and the waves, the whole of Earth, is dancing and moving about? And God is calling out the directions? Like the square dance caller, "**[God] sends forth His command to the Earth**" (Ps. 147:15). Just like the square dancers follow the caller's instructions, so "**the winds and sea obey Him**" (Mt. 8:27). The whole of Earth is doing just as God commands!

Wouldn't it be fun to see a bit of Earth's dance? Would you like to learn the steps and directions that God commands of Earth in its dance? Well, we'll need a hard-boiled egg again! (As we study God's Earth, you are probably becoming an expert boiler of eggs!)

We are not, however, going to cut open our hard-boiled egg exactly as when we studied the Earth's core. Instead this time we are going to CRACK it! Can you gently crack your hard-boiled egg on all sides? You are probably wondering why would we crack up our precious Earthly home? Who ever thought of such a wild idea? You may be surprised who did!

A long time ago, in 1858, there was a geographer named Antonio Snider-Pellegrini who believed the truth that God created the world. Antonio Snider-Pellegrini read these words in the first chapter of the Bible, "***And God said, let the waters under the heaven be gathered together into one place, and let the dry land appear: and it was so. And God called the dry land Earth; and the gathering together of the waters called the Seas: and God saw that it was good***" (Gen. 1:9-10).

When Antonio read these words, he pictured in his mind all the dry land as one mass with the entire ocean surrounding this one landmass. He drew a picture of the world like this:

Do you see how Mr. Snider-Pellegrini puzzled together South America into Africa in his drawing of Earth? And North America snuggles up into Europe? (Remember how we, too, wondered if the continents might fit together like the pieces of a giant puzzle?) Mr. Snider-Pellegrini wondered if that was how God first created the land in Genesis 1.

Then he drew a picture of the world as it is today: Now South America floats far away from Africa, separated by the fat s-shaped Atlantic Ocean. And North America lies *five thousand kilometers* (3,105 miles) away from Europe!

(By the way, this notion of a shifting, changing world is often attributed to another man, Mr. Alfred Wegner. But Mr. Wegner didn't write about the puzzle-piece continents until 1911. So really, the godly Mr. Snider-Pellegrini, wrote of it first as 1858 obviously comes before 1911!)

What happened to change our world so dramatically??!!

Like the cracked segments of your egg, geographers have come to believe that the Earth's crust is made up of cracked up sections called "plates." (So it was *God's* idea to have cracked up our Earth!) These plates, part of the Earth's crust, are like giant rafts of solid rock riding on the Earth's mantle.

When you look at the cracked shell of your egg, pretend you are looking at *all* of Earth's crust. Some of Earth's crust we can see: that is the continents rising up out of the waters. There is part of the Earth's crust that lies hidden: it is the deep, dark floor of the ocean. Both the Earth's continents and its oceans, which together make up the Earth's crust, ride on these moving, dancing plates.

Some plates are composed of only oceanic crust. Some plates are composed mainly only of continental crust. Some plates, however, are composed of both oceanic crust and continental crust. So when you picture Earth's dancing plates, imagine them as a solid rock shell which includes both dry land and the "land" underneath the oceans.

Looking at your egg, is the egg cracked all the way through to its center? Or is only the crust cracked? Earth's plates are like the shell of your egg. Like your cracked shell, the plates of the Earth's cracked crust are only riding on the Earth's mantle; the sections of crustal plates do not extend all the way down through Earth's outer or inner core.

Why don't you trace along your Earth's crust cracks with a marker? Where you have drawn lines on the cracks, that is called a boundary. A boundary is where something ends. Often times people put fences on boundaries to show where their land ends. Well, you've drawn on your egg the boundary lines between Earth's crustal plates.

The fence marking the boundary line between you and your neighbor is probably very clear; it may be a hedge of trees or maybe a straight wooden fence. The marker lines showing the boundaries between the cracked sections of your egg may be easily seen. Plate boundaries, however, are sometimes not so obvious. Plates may end in the middle of the ocean, not near land at all. In some parts of our Earth, like near the many islands of Indonesia, it is impossible to even tell where exactly the plate boundaries are because there are too many small pieces involved!

Tell the folks at home all about it!

What can you tell us about Earth's crust and its plates? (**Memory Joggers**: *who was the first to write of the puzzle-piece continents and what brought him to this realization? What are the different sections of the Earth's cracked crust called and how might you describe them? What are these plates composed of? What do they ride on? What can you tell me about plate boundaries?*)

Now gently squeeze your egg until some of your shell pieces slightly jiggle and dance about. Can you find any places on your egg where the eggshell has seperated? The Earth performs this dance where two of the plates on the Earth's crust separate or move apart. Geographers refer to this as *"divergent boundaries."* Let's call this dance step *"The Sea Floor Spread"*.

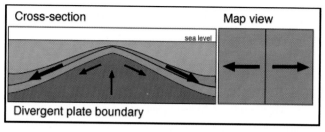

Where two of Earth's plates are separating, geographers call this a "divergent boundary." What dance step is that?   *USGS*

(Divergent means to go in different directions, which is what the earth's crust is doing when it does *"The Sea Floor Spread"*.)

Most of the separation of earth's plates is hidden deep under the floor of the ocean. As two plates separate and diverge, a rock called *magma* wells up between the two plates. Do you remember how the mantle section of the inside of our Earth was like your toothpaste, a liquid solid? Magma is the name of that liquid rock in the Earth's mantle. Magma is rock so hot that it runs like a liquid. This magma that oozes up between the two diverging plates then cools in the cold ocean water. As the magma cools, it solidifies into rock. This creates *new* Earth crust on the ocean floor. When two plates perform *"The Sea Floor Spread,"* diverging and separating, new crust is actually created on the Earth!

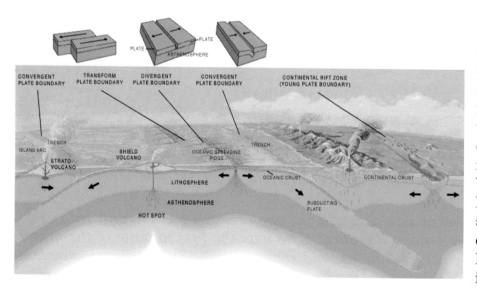

What is being created at divergent boundaries? And what is happening to Earth's crust at convergent boundaries?   *USGS*

Look at your egg. If new shell was created on your egg, that would mean you'd have more shell—but the size of your egg must still remain the same. What would happen to the old shell? Your egg can't grow *bigger*! It is a puzzler, isn't it?

Similarly, new crust *is* being created on our Earth when two plates dance *"The Sea Floor Spread."* But the size of our Earth is *not* getting any bigger. What happens to keep our Earth the same size? What happens to the old crust? Can you find places on your eggshell where two sections are colliding head on? Or one section is sliding under another? We could call this dance step of Earth "*The Continental Bend.*"

Where the plates of the Earth's crust do "*The Continetal Bend,*" smashing into each other or sliding under each other, geographers call this a "*convergent boundary.*" Convergent means to bend together. So along convergent boundaries, Earth's old crust converges and bends, either upwards or downwards. As the Earth's old crust performs "*The Continental Bend,*" this makes room on the Earth's surface for the creation of new crust. (Remember that new crust is being formed on the Earth's surface where plates are diverging and separating as they do "*The Sea Floor Spread.*")

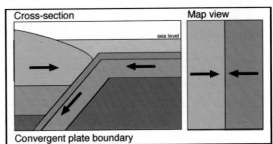

Can you see the bend of Earth's crust at "The Continental Bend" convergent boundary?
USGS

Tell the folks at home all about it!

Tell us all you've explored about Earth's dance! (**Memory Joggers:** *What can you describe about diverging plates? What can you describe about converging plates? How does "The Sea Floor Spread" and "The Continental Bend" dance together on the Earth's crust?*)

I love to squish playdough between my fingers. Or mush two rolls of playdough together. Do you know what happens when I mush two rolls of playdough together? Something like mountains bend up, or converge, in the centre!

Well, if two plates of the Earth's crust collide, and the plates are *equal* in heaviness or density, the Earth's crust folds and crumples *up* into a mountain range! It is just like those playdough rolls converge into mountains when we mush them together!

Do you remember how we learned that Earth's crust under the oceans was much thicker than Earth's crust under the continents? What happens if a *heavier* oceanic crust collides with the *lighter* continental plate? Then the oceanic crust will jerkily slip *under* the continental crust. This process is called "*subduction*";

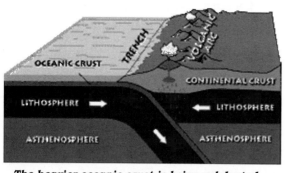

The heavier oceanic crust is being subducted under Earth's continental crust. Do you see what might happen at such a boundary?

USGS

one crustal plate is bending *under* another plate at a convergent boundary. Subduction is much like the conveyor belt at the grocery store that moves your groceries along. Imagine the ocean floor moving like that conveyor belt underneath the continental plate. Where there is subduction between the plates, there is a lot of action: earthquakes and volcanoes! *"The Continental Bend"* is certainly a dramatic Earth dance step!

Did you find any areas on your eggshell where one cracked piece did *not* slide u*nder* another section but *past* a cracked piece? When one of the Earth's plate slides and grinds past another plate, geographers call this a *"transform boundary."* How about we say that a transform boundary is Earth's *"Slippin' and Slidin"* dance step?

Have you ever tried to lay those two playdough rolls beside each other and make one slink and slide past the other? They don't move very smoothly past each other, do they? Rather, the two sections jerk and scrape along. The Earth's plates may also act like that at transform boundaries. As two plates perform the *"Slippin' and Slidin"* step past each other, what rocks our world is called an earthquake! (We'll set off on some earthquake and volcano adventures the next time we geographers meet!)

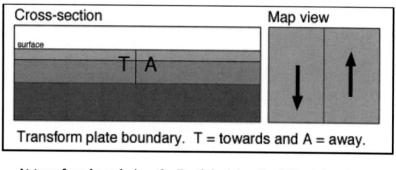

At transform boundaries, the Earth is doing the "Slippin' and Slidin' step." Can you create a transform boundary with your hands?

USGS

Tell the folks at home all about it!

*Why don't you just take a moment and share with other geographers what you've learned! (**Memory Joggers**: What is a "plate"? What is it made of? What does it ride on? What rides on top of the plates? What happens at the boundaries of plates? What is a transform boundary? A convergent boundary? A divergent boundary? What is subduction?) Good for you!*

Now did you notice where all the great action of Earth's dance happens? Yes, the action occurs on the edges of the plates, doesn't it? Nothing happens in the centre of the plates, but on the boundaries of the plates, where one plate meets another plate! This movement is called **plate tectonics.** *"Plate"* refers to slabs or rafts of the Earth's crust and *"tectonics"* comes from the Greek word *"to build."* The idea then of plate tectonics is to explain how the Earth was built. But we **know** how the Earth was built. By the very Word of God's mouth (Genesis 1). So what did all the colliding and scraping of Earth's plate build?

All these collisions, explosions and scraping remind me of two demolished cars I once saw. The vehicles were mangled messes of crushed metal. I had wondered how they ended up looking like that! Do you think the cars crept ahead bit by bit, inching very, very slowly into each other? Then, after a couple of weeks of slowly crawling into each other, the hoods of the cars finally rippled like a mountain range and the engines spewed smoke like volcanoes?! Don't you think it was more likely that the cars were careening at fast speeds, slamming head on into each other? How long then would it take to ripple the car hoods into mountains? About as fast as you can blink your eyes!

Some geographers believe that the earth's plates have been moving as slowly as those two cars crawling into each other at hardly-moving speeds, just a few inches every year, for millions and millions of years. Thus they believe it took millions of years to create mountain ranges, or to spread the continents apart.

But other geographers, like Mr. Snider-Pellegrini, think that something catastrophic and fast happened, more like the high-speed car crash! Something like a world-wide, stupendous flood!

One of the most respected geophysicists in the world, Dr. John Baumgardner, has presented a model that shows how God could have moved the Earth's continents through the Global Flood of Noah's time. Dr. Baumgardner believes that the heavy ocean floor began to sink into the softer earth below (do you remember the section of the interior of Earth called the mantle?) Then the ocean floor began to slide very quickly *underneath* the continents. Do you recall how the conveyor belt at the grocery store slides along? Imagine the ocean floor moving along like a grocery store conveyor belt on HIGH SPEED! It is thought that the ocean floor slid very quickly—about 3 ft. per second!!—underneath the continental plate. This is called *runaway* subduction! Think of it as Earth's dance step of **"The Contintental Bend"** in very, VERY fast motion!

The high-speed conveyor-belt action of the ocean floor slipping under the continents would have caused tremendous movement in the depths of Earth. These movements are thought to have ripped apart the ocean floor and the one supercontinent of Genesis 1.

Along the splits in the ocean floor Dr. Baumgardner believes that hot material, magma, from the inside of the Earth's mantle came bubbling up into the ocean water. (Do you remember what this step is called? Yes! *"The Sea-Floor Spread"*!) Can you imagine the great clouds of steam that would have erupted? Perhaps these are the *"great fountains of the deep"* of Gen. 7:11? This steam then rose into the cooler atmosphere, causing enormous clouds to rain water down upon Earth, enough rain for 40 days and 40 nights!

As the ocean floor sank deeper into the Earth's mantle, it would become hotter. As the ocean floor became hotter, it would become less heavy. This new ocean floor would then begin to rise up. If the ocean rose higher, what would happen? Yes, you can see it, can't you? The oceans would flood all the continents of the whole world! That certainly would cause the world-wide flood of Noah's time, wouldn't it!?

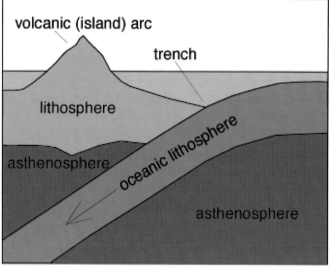

Catastrophic Plate Tectonics suggests that the Global Flood caused RUNAWAY subduction! *USGS*

The crust of the earth would have now been torn up into those huge puzzle-shape plates. The high-speed crashes of the crustal plates would have rammed up mountains. (That would be the step of *"The Contintenal Bend."*) As the new ocean floor began to cool at the end of the flood, it would get heavier and sink again. Dr. Baumgardner suggests that this sinking ocean floor would create deep ocean hollows to receive the waters retreating from the flood.

Doesn't this all sound like Psalm 104:8 where the Bible says, *"The mountains rose up; the valleys sank down"*?

Have you ever read these words on a cereal box, *"Some settling will occur"*? This means that as the cereal box has traveled to your grocery store, the cereal has shifted around and settled down in the bag. Well, you could stamp the same label on our Earth: *"Some settling will occur."* Most of the catastrophic movement of the Earth's plates occurred at the time of the Global Flood. Any movement between plates now (1-5 inches (2.5-12.5 cm) per year) is just really the plates still settling after the catastrophic Flood!

How was our Earth home "built" to look like it does today? The earth may not at all have been "built" with slow moving plate tectonics. But, perhaps, God used the *catastrophic* plate tectonics of the Flood to build up the majestic mountains and lush valleys of our Earth.

Think of the Flood as the twirling, swirling, sliding, bending, spreading, shaking MAGNIFICENT square dance.....and any movement of the Earth's plates now is simply the plates sighing and heaving after the great dance!

Are *you* sighing and heaving after all of our shaking and sliding? Together, we've just learned the dance of Earth's plates—**"The Sea-floor Spread," "The Continental Bend"** and **"Slippin' and Slidin'."** Doesn't God call Earth to perform in breath-taking ways?

So, "*come, let us sing for joy to the Lord...*
In whose hands are the depths of the earth, and the peaks of the
mountains are His also. The sea is His, for it was He who made it,
And his Hands formed the dry land...
Sing to the Lord all the Earth!" (Ps. 95-96)

POSTCARD HOME

Well, did you have fun with all of your steppin' and movin'? This was a memory that needs recording! **You can print and cut out a puzzle of the earth's plates from your CD-ROM**. *Glue it together on the front of your oversized postcard piece of cardstock! You've just puzzled all the plates of the world together!*

Now grab your pencil and draw a picture on the backside of the card of the three kinds of boundaries: divergent, convergent and transform—what can happen at each kind of boundary? Write a friend a letter on your postcard explaining how God may have dramatically moved those plates about! Add your postcard to your ring—and all of your other travels!

(Postcard templates are available on the CD-ROM in the back of your book)

Reaching Out
to His World

Do you remember the fellow that first wrote of the shifting plates of Earth, Mr. Antonio Snider-Pellegrini? From where did Mr. Pellegrini understand the idea of plate tectonics to come? Yes, from the very first chapter of the Bible, Genesis 1.

The Bible is our very word and truth from the Creator of our world Himself, God. He alone knows how the world was built. For He was there and He did it. And we believe Him! But many people do not believe what God says—or just bits and pieces of His Word.

What can you do to reach out to people who live around you who don't know how everything in our world points to the truth of our Creator God?

- You could throw a Creation Party! Every year on the March Equinox (Do you remember where Earth is in it's rotation around the sun on the March Equinox?), people the world over celebrate "Earth Day"—and you could join in with your own Creation Party! Invite some neighborhood kids over, have a slice of Earth Cake (or Mud pie) and a drink. Show a creation video that gives glory to **God** as the builder of Earth, as the Creator who has pushed up the mountains and hollowed out the oceans. Let your community know in an exciting way that **God** shifted the plates of our Earth around in a very dramatic way, not inches per year over millions of years.

- Support creation ministries like Answers in Genesis, http://www.answersingenesis.org, that believes everything the Bible says, "right from the very first verse." Subscribe to their magazine, Creation, or read it online at http://www.answersingenesis.org/creation/archive/—they have articles written specifically for young creationists –check out their "Answers for Kids" section—and then you'll have creation answers for the children in your own community!

- Why don't you pray for godly geographers and scientists right now—that they might courageously proclaim the truth of our creation and it's Creator. That they might be bold like Mr. Snider-Pellegrini and uphold every page of the Bible as truth. So that people everywhere might praise our Creator the glory due His name.

Further Explorations

In The Beginning: Catastrophic Plate Tectonics and the Genesis Flood (VHS)

(For adults or older children) American Portrait Films. 1996.

How might the continents of our world be situated as they are today? How might the Genesis Flood have dramatically transformed Earth? Learn more of Dr. John Baumgardner at Los Alamos National Laboratory model of catastrophic plate tectonics. Discover how runaway thermal subduction may have caused the breakup and flooding of Pangea, the early supercontinent.

Too-Fun-to-Resist Excursion!

DOING EARTH'S DANCE

Earth is doing it's dance and God is calling forth the steps! Are you ready for some singing and praise stepping of your own? I'll be like the square dance caller and you see if you can follow the calls!

Materials needed:
~ just a caller and a duo of geographers (or a caller can be the geographer's partner!)

Ready To Go? Let's Head Out!

~ Find a fellow geographer to be your partner.
Face each other and hold hands.
Now take several steps backwards at the same time.
Whoooa! What happened!? Did you just let go of each other's hands?!
Well, you've just danced **"The Sea Floor Spread"** that happens at **divergent plates**, when two plates rip apart!

Look at the space between you and your partner. Imagine it being filled with magma. TA DA! That's new crust just being formed on Earth's surface! (and where a volcano or earthquake could surprise! So rumble if you'd like!)

Ready for our next dancing plate step?

~ Face your geographer partner. Stand a few feet apart, with arms stretched straight out.
Reach out and touch each other's fingertips.
Now, walk towards each other.
Whooooa, again! What happened!? Did your hands and arms bend?
You just performed **"The Continental Bend"** which is involved in the bending and crumpling up of mountains between **convergent boundaries!** (Earthquakes can happen here, so shake and rattle!)

But maybe you or your partner had to let his/her arms slide beneath the arms of the other?

You've still performed **"The Continental Bend,"** but you've done the subduction move where one plate slides over and one plate slides under the other! It is still a **convergent boundary**, but the bending happens *under* instead of *up*!

If you've just done the subduction version of **"The Continental Bend,"** maybe you now want to roar and explode like a volcano? Volcanoes can occur both at a converging or diverging plate boundary, so remember to rumble when doing either **"Sea Floor Spread"** or **"The Continental Bend."** An earthquake can happen during any of the plate's movements, so shake whenever!

Ready for our last plate dance call?

~ Face your fellow geographer.
Both of you now place your hands palm to palm at waist level. Now slide one hand forward in a smooth, gentle motion. When plates are side by side each other, but there is no pressure, the movement is just like your hand movement—slow and steady.

Now, press your hands firmly together and try to slide one hand up beyond the other hand. WHOOOA, again! What happened??!!

Did your hand move forward in jerky motions? If pressure builds between the plates, the movement of Earth's plates results in earthquakes! The longer the pressure builds, the bigger the earthquake! So really shake and rattle!!! You've just performed **"Slippin' and Slidin'"** or what happens at a **transform boundary** between the Earth's plates.

117

Too-Fun-to-Resist Excursion!

PLAYING PLATE PLAY DOUGH!

Playing with play dough is always a creative experience! Can you imagine, however, what it must be like to create MOUNTAINS and pull apart the sea floor, like God does!

Materials needed:

~ play dough (or two pieces of foam rubber—whichever is most conveniently available for you)

*(Here is a recipe for the "**Best Play Dough Ever**" to make some of your own:*
Combine in saucepan*: 1 cup flour, 1/4 cup salt, 1 tsp. cream of tartar*
Add and whisk until smooth*: 1 cup water, 1 Tbsp oil, Food coloring*
Cook *over medium heat until nearly play dough is nearly set.*
Add*: 1 Tbsp. imitation vanilla extract*
Stir until vanilla is blended, then remove and knead when cool. Store in Ziploc bag or airtight container.)

Ready To Go? Let's Head Out!

~ Take two chunks of play dough and roll into a fat log shape. Now imagine that each piece is one of Earth's plates, forming the crust.

~ Press the two pieces together? What happens when the "plates" **converge**? (Do you remember what we called this "step"?) Imagine what it was like during the flood when God created some extraordinarily magnificent mountains when two plates converged!

~ Now place two pieces of play dough together and slowly move them apart. How does Earth's surface change when plates "**diverge**"? (What did we call this "step"?)

~ Roll your play dough out into another two pieces. Place the two sections together so that their sides touch. Then move the play dough pieces slowly apart in opposite directions. What happens at plate **transform** boundaries? (Do you recall what we named this "step"?)

Now, why don't you take all your play dough and create your own model of Earth after the Flood! Create some high mountains, some low sea valleys—and while you mold up your model, sing praises to God for this glorious globe He created as our home!

STRESSES, FAULTS AND EXPLOSIONS

Chapter 9

"It's not my fault!"
Do you ever say anything like that?

"I just need a break from all this stress!"
Who says that in your home?

"Oh, I think I am going to EXPLODE!"
Well, I hope no one says that!

But did you know that the Earth has lots of faults, too much stress and sometimes just explodes!? And that God can use these things for good? Now, that is worth further exploration, isn't it?

Are you ready for an Earth adventure of shaking, rattling, rolling, rumbling, and explosions? This is a geographic adventure that you will never forget!

Grab your globe of our world and let's figure out where we traveled in our last exploration of Earth. Do you recall how God used the Global Flood to crack Earth's crust into several floating plates? Those plates are still moving about and settling from the flood. Some plates are performing the *"Sea-floor Spread,"* diverging and separating. Other plates are doing the *"The Continental Bend,"* converging and bending upwards or downwards. Finally, other plates are performing *"The Slippin' and Slidin'"* at the transform boundaries where two plates slip and slide past each other.

Now that we've seen how God calls the steps of Earth's dance, let's more closely explore the rattlings and rumblings that happen between Earth's plates.

When I was younger, crowds made me feel stressed! All the jostling, pushing, pulling of all those people made me feel squashed. With all the tall and short and big and small people milling and moving about, I felt like I couldn't breathe! So a very wise person told me to wear an elastic band around my wrist. When I felt mounting pressure and stress in crowds of people, I was to pull the elastic band on my wrist. SNAP! The snapping of that elastic band released all of my building, mounting stress.

With some plates diverging and separating, other plates converging and colliding, and still others slipping and sliding, the Earth's crust feels stress too! How does Earth release all this stress that keeps growing and mounting? The Earth's crust simply SNAPS under the stress, much like the elastic band I wore around my wrist.

The crust of Earth can actually *break apart* under the stress of moving plates! This is called a *fault*. When you break something, it is your fault too, isn't it? Well, the Earth's faults are different than your faults! **Faults** are weak spots of the Earth's crust, where one part of the crust has moved against another part. Then the crust snaps and breaks apart. The crack at a *fault* usually extends no more than about 10 miles (16 km.) deep into the core of the Earth. Most faults happen where two plates meet. But some faults or cracks happen in the middle of one of Earth's plate.

"Then there came...a severe earthquake...The great city split into three parts, and the cities of the nations collapsed." Rev. 16:18-19
God has showed his power through earthquakes from the beginning of time...and will until the end of time!
USGS

Strike-slip

Normal

Thrust

Earth's 3 faults:

(1) Strike-slip, (2) normal, and (3) reverse (or thrust) faults.
USGS

When Earth's crust abruptly jolts and breaks, we feel Earth's natural release of stress through the shaking and trembling of the ground. That is what we call an **earthquake**! Earthquakes occur wherever there is a fault. Just remember that every earthquake definitely has a fault!

How many different kinds of faults or weak spots do you have? I know I certainly have many different kinds of faults, but the Earth has only three different kinds. (Wouldn't you like to have only three types of faults?) But remember, while the Earth may just have three *types* of faults, those faults can happen *all over* the entire world!

Why does the Earth have only three types of faults? This is because Earth has only *three* kinds of stresses happening at plate boundaries. (Wouldn't you like to have only 3 types of stresses?)

One type of stress occurs where the Earth is being tugged apart. Do you remember where that is? That's right: where two plates are performing **"The Sea Floor Spread,"** at divergent plate boundaries. When the Earth breaks under this kind of stress it is called a "**normal fault**."

Whoever thought a fault could be normal? You may know some people with some very abnormal, unusual faults, but geographers call any fault or crack on Earth "normal" if along the crack, one section of rock slides *downward* and *away* from another block of rock.

Look at how this earthquake rumbled along this *normal fault* in Hawaii, U.S.A. in 1975. Can you see how one part of the Earth slid *downward* and *away* from the other? Well, that is a normal fault!

(Can you butt the knuckles of both your hands together? Now, move the knuckles of one hand down and away from the other hand. There! You've just made your own version of a very small earthquake along a normal fault line!)

Do you find it stressful to crash head-on into someone? So does Earth! Where are plates crashing into each other, compressing and bending upwards or downwards? Yes! At convergent boundaries! When forces in the Earth's crust push against each other, the Earth breaks in a way called a "*reverse fault*" (or *thrust fault*).

At this normal fault in Hawaii, the ground slid downward and away! This geographer is measuring the distance of the fault. USGS

Where a river once ran quietly by, a reverse fault created this 30 ft (8 meter) waterfalls in Taiwan! NOAA

Did you think a reverse fault was when someone reversed the blame and said it was your fault when it wasn't? *Reverse faults* are actually the cracks formed where one block of rock *slides under* another block, or one block of rock is being *pushed up over* another.

At one time this river in Taiwan ran calm and quietly. An earthquake along a reverse fault line, however, created a thundering new 8 meter (30 ft.) waterfall!

(To create your own *reverse fault* line, try butting your knuckles together and pushing your two hands together. Do you see one hand slide up over the other? That is just like a mini-earthquake along a reverse fault line!)

We have now looked at two of Earth's faults: a *normal fault* which happens during the tugging apart at a divergent plate boundary, *a reverse fault* which happens during the pushing together at a convergent plate boundary.

What is Earth's third type of fault? The third fault is called a *"strike-slip fault."* Now, that may sound like when it is your fault for slipping or striking out in a baseball game, but Earth's **strike-slip faults** are the cracks between two plates that are sliding past each other. Do you remember at what kind of boundary plates slide past each other? At transform boundaries!

(Can you butt your knuckles together again? As you try to slide your knuckles *past each* other, do you see how blocks of land get caught together and lock? Pressure then builds between the two locked plates, just like the force between your two sets of knuckles. As your knuckles snap past each other, like at a *strike-slip fault,* did you feel any rumbles like an earthquake!?)

At this strike-slip fault in the country of Guatemala (pictured above), folks stand in astonishment of an earthquake that moved one half of a cement ditch over several feet! (In several places along the strike-slip fault, objects slid over more than 3 meters or 10 feet!) Isn't it amazing when God quakes our Earth! What tremendous power!

People in the country of Guatemala stand amazed by God's power at a strike-slip fault that moved a ditch several feet!
USGS

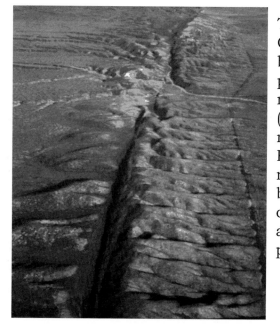

Stretching over 800 miles across the state of California, sections of the San Andreas Fault Line produce large earthquakes every 22 years!   *USGS*

The San Andreas Fault is a strike-slip fault, in California, U.S.A. It is the main boundary between the Pacific plate and North American plate. This fault slices 15 to 20 km. (9 to 12 miles) deep into the Earth, about 1,300 km. (600 miles) long, and, in places, stretches meters wide! If we stood over the San Andreas Fault, which can be as much as 25 feet (7.6 meters) wide, where the movement and stress between the plates have shattered and crushed rock, you could bend over and break apart the rocks with your bare hands! God's power truly boggles our minds!

Tell the folks at home all about it!

*Tell us all about the faults of Earth? (Yes, normally we would not discuss the faults or sins of others, but Earth's faults are a bit different!) (**Memory Joggers**: What is a fault and how many different types of faults does Earth have? Describe a "**normal**" fault. Talk with your hands! (That means, use your hands to demonstrate what your are explaining!) What happens at a "**reverse**" fault? Where do normal and reverse faults occur? Can you show with your hands and describe with your words a "**strike-slip**" fault? What did you discover about one strike-slip fault, the San Andreas Fault?)*

We've now discovered Earth's three kinds of faults—*normal, reverse and strike-slip.* We have learned how the Earth releases stress through rumbling earthquakes! But sometimes the Earth reacts to pressure in a more EXPLOSIVE way! Are you ready for a dangerous escapade into some hot territory along plate boundaries?

I once knew a little boy who had full-blown temper tantrums if he didn't get what he wanted. His chubby cheeks would flame fiery red, he'd tightly clench his fists and then jump up and down in a rage! Have you ever shook a can of soda pop and then opened the can? Didn't a stream of pop erupt and spew about everywhere? Well, that little boy looked like a shaken can of pop about ready to explode! The little fellow was *"hot under the collar"* which is one way of saying he was angry and needed to retire to his room to cool down.

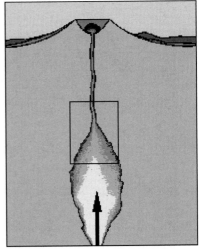

The pressure in the magma chamber explodes into a volcano!   *USGS*

But Earth doesn't cool down as quietly. Instead, the way the Earth cools down is to ERUPT dramatically in a **volcano**!

What exactly is a volcano? You could say that a volcano is a vent or chimney for Earth to cool down. If you could crawl down one of these vents, below the Earth's surface, you would find very hot areas several miles underground where there are pools, not pools of water (even though you certainly would be hot enough for a swim!), but pools of magma and hot gases.

Mauna Loa, the largest volcano in the world, takes up half the size of the island of Hawaii and is one of the most active volcanoes in the world, erupting 15 times since 1900!   *USGS*

Magma is a liquid rock that forms when the lower part of the Earth's crust and upper part of the mantle begin to melt. Not as dense as the solid rock that surrounds it, the magma or liquid rock begins to rise. The rising magma looks for a weak spot or fault line in the Earth's crust to pool into. Over time a large pocket of melted, liquid rock is formed, called a ***magma chamber.***

Gases are released slowly from this melting rock. These gases build up pressure within the magma chamber. The pressure of magma deep within the Earth's mantle builds and builds in certain places, just like that naughty little boy's anger grew and grew. Finally the Earth's surface rips open into a volcano, which may spew out magma, ashes and gases—just like that little boy erupted into tears and hollering!

Happily, not all children explode in full blown-temper tantrums like that little boy that I knew. Did you ever know someone who expressed frustration not with a violent explosion but with a very quiet flow of hot tears?

As all children are not the same, neither are all volcanoes. There are actually three kinds of volcanoes, all of which behave a bit differently. It all depends on what kind of materials they erupt.

If the magma that erupts from a volcano is thin and runny, the gases within the magma escape easily. Then there is no thunderous explosion, just a flow of magma or lava. (Once magma erupts unto the Earth's surface, we change its name and call it ***lava*.**)

One quiet volcano such as this one, Mauna Loa, in Hawaii, U.S.A., is the largest volcano in the world. Another shield volcano in Hawaii, Kilauea, has been oozing out lava continuously since 1983, over 25 years!

Lava is terrifyingly hot! Watch your feet!   *USGS*

If you would like a close-up glance of such a lava flow, you'll have to crowd in with other tourists from all over the world. (Have a look, but don't reach out to scoop up a handful of the lava. Lava can reach staggeringly burning temperatures of 1,290-2,280F (700 to 1250C)! Remember to keep an eye on the sole of your shoes! If your boot soles are held on only by glue, and the glue starts to melt, it's time to beat a hasty retreat off the lava!)

Mount Pinatubo's largest and most monstrous eruption, lasting 3 whole hours, spewed ash 21 miles (34 km) up into Earth's atmosphere and damaged more than 73,000 homes!   *USGS*

These volcanoes may be rather quiet, but they are Earth's largest volcanoes with their long gentle, slopes from the many lava-flows that ooze out over great distances. Actually, this kind of hushed volcano is called a "***shield volcano***" since it looks like a massive, upturned warrior's shield. (Think of these volcanoes as quiet giants crying lava flows and clinging to their huge shields.)

If the magma that erupts from a volcano is not thin and runny but cooler, thick and sticky, like toothpaste, the gases in the magma get trapped. These trapped gases act much like your shaken pop can. The shaking motion forms bubbles which increases the pressure inside your can. Now what happens when you open your pop can? All the gases and pop gush out with explosive speed all over you! Well, that is the same way God forms some thunderous, violent volcanoes!

These explosive volcanoes produce steep layers of ash and lava. (One such explosive volcano as this one, Mt. Pinatubo in the Philippines, erupted so much ash during its 1991 explosion that you would need a box, 2.5 miles (10 km.) long, high and wide to hold all the ash!) Such volcanoes are called "***composite volcanoes.***" "***Composite***" means to be made up of parts. That perfectly describes composite volcanoes since they are made up of the two parts of lava and ash, like layers of cake and frosting on a very tall cake! Six out of every ten volcanoes is a composite volcano.

When composite volcano Mt. St. Helen erupted in 1980, it blew 1,314 feet (400 m) of mountain rock off the top! Within minutes, a massive plume of ash thrust 11 miles (19 km) into the sky. Wind carried about 540 million tons of ash from the explosion across 35,500 sq miles, (57,000 square km) of the Western United States. *USGS*

Composite volcanoes, such as this one, Mt. St Helens, in Washington, U.S.A., stand as some of Earth's most beautiful—but dangerous—mountains! (Think of these composite volcanoes as dangerously explosive Goliaths who just want to have their cake and eat it too!)

Tell the folks at home all about it!

Tell us about a shield volcano—what kind of magma does it erupt? What does a shield volcano look like and what would it be like to visit one? Can you describe a composite volcano and what kind of magma it erupts? What else have you discovered about volcanoes?

We've toured **shield volcanoes** with its lava flows and steep **composite volcanoes** with its layers of ash and lava. Are you ready to explore the third kind of volcano? And if you are tiring, be encouraged. This last kind of volcano is Earth's smallest type.

You may have known a child who grew explosively angry, very quickly...but then calmed down to play happily. Well, that rather describes the third type of volcano called *"cinder cone volcanoes."* Cinder cone volcanoes are the simplest type of volcano. Gas-charged lava erupts violently into the air, then breaks into smaller fragments. These fragments of lava become hard, or solidify. The chunks then fall down as dark volcanic rock around the vent or chimney of the volcano. These cinder cone volcanoes are shaped

Cinder cone volcanoes are shortest of the volcanoes, rarely rising more than 1,640 ft (500 m) above their surroundings. Cinder cones commonly erode rapidly unless further eruptions occur. *USGS*

like an oval-cone and rise only about 1,000 feet. Here a cinder cone volcano, in the country of Papua New Guinea, sends an eruption column into the sky.

While cinder cone volcanoes may not rise very high, they certainly can rise fast! One cinder cone volcano in Mexico called Paricutin rose up 2 to 2 ½ meters in just one day, right under the very feet of a corn farmer named Pulido! The next day, the cone in Pulido's cornfield had grown to 30 feet high. (That is about 5 times taller than the height of your Dad!) And the cone was violently hurling out lava! When Pulido went to bed that night, the cone had grown yet another 120 feet and brightly glowing pieces of lava were shooting 1,000 feet up into the darkness! That was the beginning of the 424 meter high cinder cone volcano that grew up in Pulido's cornfield and spewed out lava for the next nine years, covering 25 square kilometers of land! (So think of a cinder cone volcano as quick growing, feisty little fellows hurling hot rocks of lava into the air!)

Now, don't worry that a volcano might sprout up anytime right under your feet! Volcanoes do not rise up randomly across our Earth, but most volcanoes—6 out of every 10—occur at the boundaries between Earth's plates, the same place where earthquakes may also shake us up.   Earth actually has its own ring. It is a ring, or circle, of active volcanoes called the **"Pacific Ring of Fire."** Over half of the world's spewing, brewing, fuming volcanoes explode around this "ring of fire" because crustal plates are scraping, colliding and buckling.

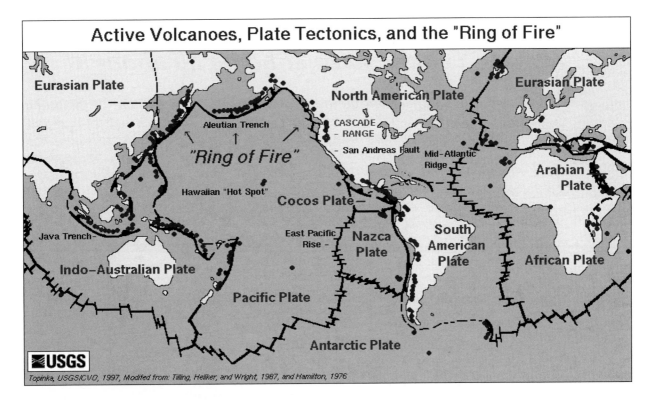

Shaped like a horseshoe, the Pacific Ring of Fire is home to 90% of Earth's earthquakes and 81% of the world's volcanoes. Do you see the hot red spots lined up on the plate boundaries?

How do converging, slipping Earth plates create an event as spectacular as a volcano?   Picture in your mind the heavier crust of Earth under the ocean slipping under the lighter continental plate. (Do you remember what this plate movement is called? Yes! This is referred to as **subduction**.) As the ocean plate slips along, water from the ocean makes the plates slippery like oil, allowing one plate to slide under another. This water actually lowers the melting point of the overlying rocks. Can you then see the rocks beginning to melt? The hot, melting rocks are called **magma**. When the magma pushes up through the Earth's crust, the Earth has another volcano! This type of subduction volcano can punch up out of the ocean, creating whole islands!

127

Volcanoes also spring up where the Earth is doing the **"Sea-floor Spread,"** separating apart at divergent plate boundaries. The magma pushes to the surface and erupts. Geographers estimate that there are over 10,000 volcanoes in the ocean. Geographers never see these eruptions as they occur deep in the dark depths of the water!

Only 5% of volcanoes actually happen in the middle of the Earth's plates, at what geographers call hotspots. (It sounds like when that little boy was hot under the collar, doesn't it?) At hot spots, the searing hot magma melts through the plate and erupts into a volcano!

Tell the folks at home all about it!

Haven't you had quite the adventure? Tell us about it! (**Memory Joggers**: *What makes cinder cone volcanoes different from shield or composite volcanoes? Tell us what you discovered about the Paricutin volcano. What do you picture for each the shield, composite and cinder-cone volcanoes? Where do most volcanoes happen? Describe the creation of a volcano due to subduction)*

After exploring all of the commotion of volcanoes and earthquakes that occur at plate boundaries, you may be scratching your head as to why God made the Earth with these shifting plates causing earthquakes and volcanoes! The Bible says, **"He looks at the earth, and it trembles, he touches the mountains and they smoke"** (Ps. 104:32). As God makes all things work together for good in our lives, God can make good come out of even dangerous and destructive volcanoes that grow up at places like plate boundaries.

Would you like to farm in Java, Indonesia at the base of the active Sunduro volcano? Look at the rich soil! *USGS*

Did you know that some of the most fertile, productive soils on Earth have formed from the breakdown and weathering of rocks from volcanoes? In Hawaii, the lush growth of new plants on rich soil can happen as fast as a few hundred years after a volcano eruption. If you traveled back in time and history, you'd find the Greeks and Romans settled on fertile, volcanic soil. And if you traveled today to the shadows of looming, active volcanoes in Indonesia, you'd find farmers growing the very best rice in the country.

Do you recall how hot pools of magma exist under volcanoes? Well, people can use the heat from the magma to create energy. This energy is called "**geothermal energy.**" "**Geo**" means earth and "**thermal**" means heat, so geothermal energy is the earth's heat. This photo shows two geothermal power plants at the largest geothermal development in the world, in California, U.S.A.. In Iceland where there are 22 active volcanoes, most houses are heated by this geothermal energy. In some Icelandic cities you would find even the sidewalks are heated in wintertime! I know a man who once made very good use of the heat generated by volcanoes: he fried an egg right there on the rocky slope of the volcano!

The Geysers, the world's largest geothermal power plant, is in a volcanic area in northern California *USGS*

When the hot magma hardens under an old, inactive volcano, guess what you might find? If you drilled a mine deep into the Earth at such a place, you would find most of the metallic minerals mined in the world, such as copper, gold, silver, lead, and zinc. Who would have thought such gems lay deep under volcanoes in hardened magma? Don't you agree that God works all things together for His glorious good?

Yes, God even works good through the most thunderous, monstrous volcanoes, through the most ground-rumbling earthquakes, through the scraping and grinding and crunching of Earth's plates....and through people like you and me with too much stress, too many faults and who are sometimes too hot under the collar!

POSTCARD HOME

Well, we've experienced the grand adventures of way over the Earth, of way down under the Earth, and now we've made our way back through all the exciting moving and shifting of Earth! Time to write a postcard, don't you think? Draw a picture of the three different kinds of earthquake faults....and a picture of the three different kinds of volcanoes! Then can you write about the stresses of Earth? And how it sometimes even explodes? Remember to include how God uses even these things for good! Place it on your ring with postcards from your other travels! Oh, what a tale you will have to tell!

(Postcard templates are available on the CD-ROM in the back of your book)

Reaching Out
to His World

Imagine lying in your bed early in the morning. The sun still has not peeked up on the horizon. All is dark. And your bed begins to shake. Violently. But only for 20 seconds. Twenty seconds does not seem very long. But in 1995 when the earth shook for only 20 seconds, in Kobe, a city in Japan, the ground moved back and forth up to 50 centimeters and up to 1 meter up and down! And over 300,000 people's homes were destroyed.

Why did the Earth shake so? Three of Earth's plates meet near the coast of Japan. One of these denser oceanic plates is being subducted beneath a lighter continental plate, very near to the city of Kobe. As the plates rumbled, the earth shook breaking water pipes, crumbling highways, toppling buildings into the streets.

Then the Earth quieted and settled. But families were left with unsettling circumstances: Clean water was in short supply for months. Parents lived out of tents or cars even though it was winter because they had no place to live. And children didn't school for many months.

What can you do to reach out to aid moms and dads, brothers and sisters, grandmas and grandpas who experience earthquakes every year in our home called Earth?

Those who study how the plates of our Earth move, predict that on average 17 major earthquakes occur each year somewhere in the world, one of which will be very disastrous. Jesus knew such earthquakes would happen and told us so (Mt 24:6-8). God calls us to show His love when it does. When you hear of an earthquake, you can:

- **Pray.** Pray that people will have homes to sleep in, that they will have food, that they will not worry and have a measure of peace, knowing that even in this, God loves them. Your prayers can wrap a family in God's love even when they are left without a home. It is something you can do, wherever you are.

- **Donate**. Help an organization that is bringing aid to the earthquake region. Give coats, blankets, and money to charities that are sending supplies. Do what you can. Jesus asks us to.

God can use even an earthquake for good, like when He caused an earthquake to break open the prison and free Paul and Silas (Acts 16). How might God want to use you to bring good to an earthquake zone today?

Further Explorations

Volcanoes and Earthquakes: A Child's Guide to God's Power beneath our feet
by Michael Carrol
(Gr. 2-5) What is happening beneath your feet? What is the ultimate force moving through all of Creation? Our breathtaking and Glorious God!

Mount St. Helens: Explosive Evidence for Catastrophe (VHS) *Institute for Creation Research*
(for adults or older children) Join Christian scientist, Dr. Austin, as he tours you through visually captivating photography of volcanoes and its ripple effect throughout the environment.

Voice of the Volcano *Answers in Genesis*
Incorporating research from Mount St. Helens, this comic book presents a creationist perspective.

Earthshake: Poems from the Ground Up *by Lisa Westeberg Peters*
(Gr. 1-6) Weave poetry with geology in these 22 exuberant poems exploring tectonic plates, lava, strata, and fossils. Endnotes explain the flights of fancy in geological terms. In the poem "Continental Promises," Africa and South America dash off brief love notes to each other ("Dear Africa/ Stay close!") while the endnotes offer thoughts on continental drift.

Eyewitness: Volcano and Earthquake *by Susanna Van Rose*
(Gr. 4-7) Brilliant graphics and informative captions introduce readers to some of earth's most spectacular phenomena. Learn how earthquakes and volcanoes occur; be fascinated with stunning photographs such as a Philippine town dusted in ash by Mount Pinatubo. A most effective introduction.

Hill of Fire *by Thomas P. Lewis*
(Gr. 1-3) "El Monstruo!" Pablo's father's quiet, predictable world dramatically changes one afternoon when the ground below his feet hisses, smokes and opens wide to swallow up his plow! Who ever would have guessed that a volcano is erupting right in the middle of his cornfield!?

Volcano: The Eruption and Healing of Mount St. Helens *by Patricia Lauber*
(Gr. 4-8) Vivid photography integrates with clear text to lead readers through the staggering eruption of Mt. St. Helens, the geological causes for the eruption, and how new environments have slowly emerged from the after-math. A thought-provoking read.

Into the Volcano: A Volcano Researcher at Work *by Donna O'Meara*
(Gr. 4-6) Follow a typical day in the life of volcano researcher Donna O' Meara, complete with melting running shoes, a rain of foot-ball-size globs of lava, toxic gases, airborne ash, and hypothermia! Run with her through clouds of scalding steam and hurricane-force winds just to get to peer into a volcano's cone. This treacherous, extreme journey to volcanoes in Hawaii, Costa Rica, Guatemala and Italy is simply unforgettable!

131

Too-Fun-to-Resist Excursion!

WATER QUAKES

Earthquakes happen along fault lines—and some of those fault lines run along the floor of the ocean. What happens when an earthquake occurs on the ocean floor?

Instead of tumbling down buildings, an earthquake on the ocean floor moves the water above it, creating a monstrously huge wave. Such a gigantic wave, the result of such an ocean floor earthquake, is called a **tsunami**. Can you imagine a tsunami, 100 miles (160 km.) long, come rushing upon you at speeds of 500 miles (805 km.) per hour, rising, black and ominous, 100 feet (30m.) up out of the water?

In 2004, a devastating tsunami slammed into Southeast Asia, killing hundreds of thousands of people and leaving millions of families with no homes. This picture shows how high the tsunami wave grew after that earthquake. You could simulate a wee earthquake in your bathtub and watch for a small tsunami. While you do, think about how terrifying it might be to survive a real-life tsunami.

Materials:

~ water in your bathtub
~ two bricks
~ toy boat (or something that floats)
~ wax paper (about 2 ft. or 60 cm. long)
~ string (2 sections about 1 ft. long or
30 cm. each)

Thousands of homes were entirely washed away in an Indian Ocean tsunami in December 2004.   USGS

Ready To Go? Let's Head Out!

~ Lay your sheet of wax paper on the bottom of the tub. Then tie one section of string around one end of one of the bricks. Then tie the other section of string around the other end of the same brick. There—you have just made a kind of chain or leash for your one brick.

~ Lay both bricks, side by side, touching, on top of the wax paper. Place your toy boat over the center of the two bricks.

~ Now fill your tub with water, just covering the bricks by about ¾ of an inch of water (or 2 cm.). With a quick jerk, pull your two strings, so as to move the one brick. This simulates an earthquake on the ocean floor.

~ What happened on the water's surface? Did you see the beginnings of a small-scale tsunami?

Too-Fun-to-Resist Excursion!

EXPLOSIVE VOLCANO

Have you ever accidentally squeezed your drinking box? Well, that is much like some volcano! Imagine the juice is molten magma, steam and gas under massive pressure. The only way to release that pressure within Earth is up through a "straw" to the surface. But the straw is plugged with cooled magma. The volcano may then pop its plug—in a violent outburst!

To think that the Earth under our feet may explode is hard to imagine! But every year about 50 volcanoes do just that. Geographers and scientists study volcanoes so they can warn families to flee before the impending eruption of gases, hot ash and lava. For even the gases from certain kinds of volcanoes can be poisonous and deadly. The gas, hydrogen sulfide, smells like rotten eggs and burns eyes and throats and can even eat through your clothing!

You might simulate your own small volcano. But remember—experiencing a real volcano would be very dangerous and very frightening.

Materials

~ brown craft paint (optional)
~ 1 cup of water
~ 2 cups flour
~ 1 cup salt
~ styrofoam cup

~ small medicine cup
~ explosive recipe: 1 Tbsp Plaster of Paris, Tbsp water, few drops dish soap, red food coloring
~ baking soda

Ready To Go? Let's Head Out!

~ Stir a bit of brown paint into 1 cup of water. Mix the water paint with 2 cups of flour and 1 cup of salt. Knead it into a smooth dough, adding more flour or water if you think you need to change the consistency.

~ Now flatten your ball of dough into a large, flat patty.

~ Cut out the entire bottom piece of your Styrofoam cup. Using your cup as a cutter, cut out a hole in the center part of your dough patty.

~ Turning your cup and your dough patty upside down, now shape the dough around your cup to form a volcano. What kind of volcano have you shaped –a shield volcano, a composite volcano, or a cinder-cone volcano?

~ See if you can take a small medicine cup and insert it into the top of your volcano. (Use a bit of extra dough to secure it.)

~ Now mix 1 tbsp of Plaster Paris, 1 tbsp of water, a few drops of dish soap and red food color into your medicine cup.

~ To begin your eruption, stir in 1 tsp of baking soda.

What happened?! Maybe you would now like to be a newspaper reporter. Grab a pencil and paper and write a report for your local newspaper about what creates a volcano and what it might be like to experience a real power of a volcano.

(Easier "Volcano": Simply take a tube of red icing/frosting (or a tube of toothpaste) and poke a hole with a needle or a pin in the side of the tube. What happens when you squeeze the tube? Similarly, the pressure builds under the Earth's crust, eventually forcing hot lava up through the Earth's crust. If you poke holes in a straight line all around the tube, you'll create a series of "eruptions" along your own wee Ring of Fire.)

GOD'S GREAT SIGNS AND IMAGINARY LINES

Chapter 10

(Pack an orange, cutting knife and apple with you as we head out on this geographical adventure!)

I once read of a sailor, out in the endless rocking ocean, who used a big stick to find his way back home! How did the stick direct him home? Actually, that stick was a very unique kind of picture, showing him where he was! As he paddled along in his boat, he carved notches in that stick. Whenever the land jutted out into the water, he carved a bit of wood off his stick to make a jut. When the coastline curved away to make a bay, he too carved a curve on his stick. When he decided to turn for home, he just counted the number of notches on his stick. The number of notches was the number of bays he had to oar past before he found himself back at home-sweet-home!

Wanderers have been drawing pictures of their travels since God first created the world: notches on sticks, sketches on bark, lines in the dirt, shells tied to nets. Each of these pictures is a kind of "*map.*" Maps are pictures of journeys, drawings of part of our home of Earth, drawn as if one were a seeing our home as if flying overhead like a bird. It is easier to draw a map in some ways than a picture, for in a map we do not have to mark the heights of things, but only their edges and distances from other things.

The distance between things on a map is very different from the distance between things on the actual ground. And so, always look at the scale of your map!

The distances between things on a map are marked by what we call a **scale**. A **scale** tells you how the distance between things on the map picture compares to the *actual* distance between the things on the ground. When studying map pictures, always first study the scale to understand the relationship between the map distances and the distances on the ground.

Men in the Bible drew such map pictures of the things on the ground where they lived. The Biblical book of Joshua reads: **"As the men started on their way to _map_ out the land, Joshua instructed them, "Go and make a survey of the land and write a description of it"** (Joshua 18:8 italics added NIV). Joshua was telling those men to draw a picture and write a story, describing how the land rolled down and away...then stretched out into calm plains...then rose into bluffs and how the rivers curled its way through the lands and back again. Yes, very long ago, these Israelites were exploring, discovering....and drawing maps.

Perhaps their map looked much like the oldest map we have ever found, a picture of two hills with a river cutting through it. Right in the middle of the map is a picture of a farm belonging to a man from Babylon named Azala. Azala probably didn't think we'd still have the map of his farm thousands of years later for the map was crudely drawn with a sharp-pointed stick over 2,300 years *before* the birth of Jesus. Neither was the map drawn on paper, but rather a big clump of mud! Dried into a hard tablet of clay, Azala's farm map is a picture of a part of our Earth home.

That Babylonian mapmaker who drew the map of land around Azala's farm, and the sailor map-carver—and you—all look at pictures, maps, to know current location, how to get where to a place, and then how to get back. Can you place a globe in front of you, rotated to the continent of Australia? Imagine that you are standing on a farm too, in the outback of Australia. (Look at Australia on your globe.) Then see how you would travel to visit another farm in Europe—WAIT! You had to turn the globe, didn't you? It's very hard to look at both the drawing of Australia and Europe at the same time, isn't it? When your map is shaped like the Earth, like a sphere, you can't look at the picture of all the continents, or

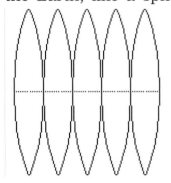

rooms, in our home at the same time. You can only see half of them at a time. So mapmakers needed to make flat pictures of the whole of Earth. (Yes, it also would be much easier to carry flat maps when out exploring the world than lugging a globe around under your arm!) Let's pull that orange out of our knapsacks and together we'll be cartographers and make flat picture maps of our Earth.

Cutting your orange peel like this, creates "gores"-- much like peeling the spherical picture of earth off a globe and laying the picture map flat.

Mapmakers are called **cartographers**. **"Cartos"** comes from the Greek word that means "leaf of paper." And we've already learned when studying the word "geo**graphy**" that the root word for **"grapher"** means "to write" in the Greek. So think of cartographers carrying around a leaf of paper to write where they are at in the world.

Hold up your orange and imagine it as a globe of our world. (You can draw on the continents with a marker, if you'd like to.) Have an adult geographer make a shallow cut with a knife into the skin of your orange from the top to the bottom of your orange. Now carefully begin to work at peeling your orange, keeping the peel in one piece if you can.

136

Gerhard Kremer Mercator, born in 1512, used the same skills as a teacher of mathematics to draw accurate maps.

Now try to flatten your orange peel out as best you can. How does your map of the world look compared to when it was wrapped around in a sphere? Do you have any ideas how you can make your peel lay flat? If you make some cuts or "**gores**" in your peel, like this, you may find that your peel lies better. Cartographers did just such a thing with their globes too. Do you see, however, the big gaps that were left on their maps! Who wants gaps in their maps?

Gerhard Kremer certainly didn't! Mr. Kremer was a cartographer in the 1500's whose map name was "Mercator." Mercator was very good at his math, and he figured out a way to project or "stretch" the ball shape map of Earth from a globe into a map the shape of a can. (Look at a globe. Now, imagine the map standing up into a can shape.) Then he cut the can shape (or cylinder) map and flattened it into a map to lie on the table! There, flat maps—with no gaps! (There may be no gaps now on maps, but Mercator's stretching makes the island of Greenland, northeast of North America, look much larger than it actually is. Greenland really is less than one third the size of the United States.) If you look carefully at the small print around the border on one of your maps, you might even actually see Mercator's name, giving him credit for the flat map and his good math!

Are you ready to eat your orange now? While you are eating your orange, think about that Babylonian cartographer drawing Azala's farm on his mud clump. What if you took his little mud map of Azala's farm and you very carefully stuck it onto a big beach ball? Then, what if you pretended the beach ball was a globe of our Earth. Can you describe to someone exactly where Azala's farm is on Earth? How far north or south, east or west—from WHERE? It's rather a predicament, isn't it? A map of Azala's farm is of no use to you if you don't know how to tell anyone where on Earth his farm actually *is*!

Can you identify any of the countries in Mercator's map of Europe?

We've had grand adventures up through Earth's atmosphere, down through Earth's core and shaking and shifting about on Earth's plates. But if we are now going to haul on our backpacks, grab our cameras and head out to explore the mountains and valleys, the deserts and oceans and everywhere in between in

God's grand home for us, we are going to have to know where on Earth we are—and how to get back home in time for dinner!

Have you ever been lost near your home? Or out on the highway with your parents? What do you look for? A sign! A sign that tells you where you are or what direction to go to get where you want to be! Did you know that God has given all of Earth some wonderful signs? Signs that help us to always find our way around Earth! Hear what God says: **"Let there be lights in the expanse of the sky to separate the day from the night, and let them serve as signs"** (Genesis 1:14).

God has made lights, the stars and the sun, like big signs way up in the sky telling us where we are, so we don't get lost!

Stars are God's signs for us here on Earth. God knows all the stars by name. And there are so many we can't even count them all! Scientists can only guess that there are approximately 1,000,000,000,000,000,000,000 stars in our universe! That is a lot of stars—and names! Doesn't God's magnificence take your breath away?

One hundred and forty years before Jesus was even born, there lived a Greek named Hipparchus, who was a scientist studying the signs God had placed way up in the sky. From the placement of the stars and the sun up in the sky, Hipparchus drew lines on a map to figure out where places were here down on Earth.

Hipparchus studies God's night sky signs to develop a grid for a map of Earth, aiding in determining locations on Earth.

How can lines on a map be helpful to find out where you are? Well, I know some boys who spend evenings before the fire playing a game called *"Battleship."* The boy with a sprinkle of freckles calls out, "B5." The boy with a crooked smile locates B on one side of his gameboard, then 5 at the bottom of the board. Then he traces the B line with one finger and the 5 line with another finger and where the two lines meet and his two fingers bump into one another, that is the point, or coordinate, on the gameboard's ocean that is named B5. Then the crooked-smiling boy calls out, "HIT!" A battleship has been discovered at the coordinate of B5! Such a concept is exactly what you need on your beach ball with its mud map: a grid or criss-cross of equally spaced horizontal and vertical lines. Each line would be named a certain number, just like some roads have number names. Then a

Ptolemy, around 100 A.D., wrote a famous work of geography, Geographia, in which he covered the earth with a gird so he could easily assign co-ordinates to places on our globe.

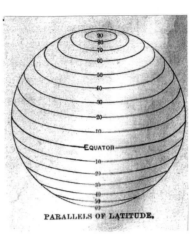

PARALLELS OF LATITUDE.

Parallels of Latitude, imaginary lines running parallel to the equator, enable us to tell how far north or south a place on Earth is from the equator.

geographer could call out, "30 North and 90 West!" You could then trace down the line on your beach ball globe named 90 West and across the line named 30 North, and at the coordinate of 30 North and 90 West, there you would find your mud map of that Babylonian town!

Now, of course, these lines didn't and don't exist on the actual ground of Earth. They are merely imaginary lines that are drawn on globes and maps based on proper measurements taken from God's signs in the sky, the sun and stars.

Another Greek worked on Hipparchus' grid, a famous geographer named Ptolemy, born about 100 years after the time of Jesus Christ. Ptolemy called the imaginary lines that ran east-west on maps the *"parallels of latitude."* *"Latitude"* refers to an angle of distance, measured from the equator to your position on Earth, telling you how far *north* or *south* you have traveled. (Remember, although the lines of latitude run *east-west*, they measure how far *north* or *south* you've journeyed.) *"Parallel"* means that the distance between two lines remains the same. Lines of latitude run parallel to each other as they circle the globe in rings and are often even referred to just as *"parallels."*

Now, how do geographers determine their position of latitude from God's signs in the sky? Imagine that you are a captain of a ship, sailing the wild seas. To figure out where in the world's latitude you were at, you'd stand on board the deck of your ship and look up into the twinkling night sky to locate a star, like the North Star. Then, by using a tool called a *sextant*, you could figure out the angle formed between your sighting of the North Star and the horizon.

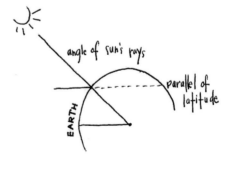

Imagine yourself standing at a point on the Earth and observing the North Star --- or the Noontime Sun. God's sky sign is at an angle above the horizon. The angle that the center of the Earth to you, out to directly over your head—the angle that makes is your position of latitude! A sextant determines the angle the sun's rays make with the horizon. Then, when one subtracts that angle from 90 degrees (the point of the Poles), one arrives at their degree of latitude!

(The **horizon** is that magnificent half-circle line created by the sky meeting the land or sea.) Perhaps you measure an angle of 40 degrees between the horizon and the North Star. That angle is the same as the angle formed at the center of the Earth. It is this angle that is your position of **LATITUDE**!

You are like sailors all down through the centuries, following God's sky signs:

> **Sea Fever** by John Masefield
>
> *I must go down to the sea again*
> *To the lonely sea and sky*
> *And all I ask is a tall ship*
> ***And a star to steer her by.***

A sextant is used to determine the position of latitude from God's signs in the sky.

Sail on! Remember that latitude refers to an ***angle*** of distance! Angles are measured in what we call ***degrees***. Thus when geographers refer to a position of latitude, they say how many ***degrees*** north or south.

Tell the folks at home all about it!

*Put in your own words what you have discovered! (**Memory Joggers**: What does latitude mean? What does it measure? What does parallel mean? How would you find your position of latitude?)*

You've just discovered how far north or south you are from—well, from where? While you now know your position of latitude, you still need a starting line of latitude-to know how far north or south you are from WHERE!

Ptolemy thought the ***equator*** should be the obvious "start" line of latitude, since it is the exact midpoint between the North and South Pole, and the equator is where the sun, one of God's signs, appears almost directly overhead year round. The equator, then, is the perfect parallel to call the zero (0) degree line of latitude.

Galloping all over the globe works up an appetite, so why don't you pull out a big red apple, and after some geographic discussion, you can enjoy! (But no biting into your apple until we understand this business of latitudes!) These parallel lines of latitude are much like if you laid that big red apple on its side. The stem would be like the North Pole and the bottom core like the South Pole. Now, cut your apple exactly in half; that would be the equator, the parallel of latitude named zero degrees. One half of your apple you could call the northern half or hemisphere of Earth. The other half of your apple you could call the southern half or hemisphere, of Earth.

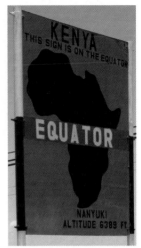

Take your northern hemisphere apple half into your hand and look at the stem. That stem at the top of your apple half is like the North Pole, the point we call 90 degrees North latitude. (We say the North Pole is at 90 degrees north because the North Pole lies at a 90 degree *angle* to the equator.) If you now drew lines on your apple on the *angle*, as pictured, then cut the apple into slices *parallel* to the equator, cutting from the *angle*, those slices would be just like the parallels of latitude!

This sign in Kenya marks where the imaginary, man-made line of the equator rings the earth!

Now, geographers obviously don't draw lines of latitude on apples but on maps. On their maps, geographers draw each degree of the imaginary parallels of latitude sixty-nine miles from the next degree of latitude. Geographers have numbered each of these degrees of parallels of latitude, just like those boys named their lines in battleship.

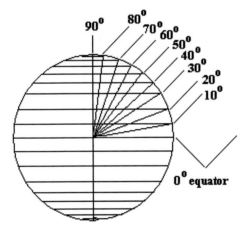

Each parallel of latitude is based on the angle created by one of God's signs in the sky and the center of Earth. We mark the center of Earth by the imaginary line of the equator. If the Equator is zero degrees, the North and South Pole create 90 degree angles to the equator. So the North Pole's position of latitude is 90 degrees North, and the South Pole's position of latitude is 90 degrees south Latitude is the angle between any point on the Earth's surface and the equator!

As geographers and sailors often sing songs as they travel along, why don't you sing this little jingle about latitude to sing as you chomp into your apple? (To the tune of "*Wheels on the Bus*"):

"I'm climbing the ladder of latitudes, latitudes, latitudes, I'm climbing the ladder of latitudes, north and south from the equator".

Doesn't the word "*latitude*" remind you of the word "*ladder*"? Now you can always remember that the parallels of latitude run the same way as rungs on a ladder and when you know your position of latitude, you know how far north or south you are from the equator!

141

Tell the folks at home all about it!

Tell us about your latitude adventures! (**Memory Joggers**: *What is the equator? What degree of latitude do we call it? Can you explain how you cut up your apple into "degree of latitude?" How far apart is each degree of latitude when marked on a map?*)

I once knew a lady who had rings—many—on each of her fingers, on both hands. When she talked her hands would flutter about her, her fingers flashing gold and silver. I asked her about her rings. While all of her rings were precious to her, she noted that several of her rings were very important to her, like her wedding ring, her grandmother's ring, and her engagement ring.

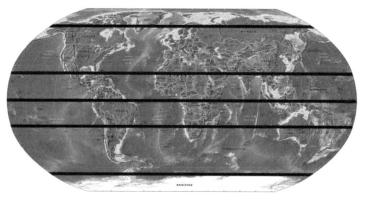

Earth too has many rings, not silver and gold rings, but rings of latitude. Of all those rings of latitude, there are five rings that are very important. Shall we have Earth tell us about her important rings?

Can you name the five most important rings of latitude that circle the Earth? What else do you now know about each of these lines or latitude?

We've already learned about one of the Earth's major rings of latitude, the Equator. This is the zero degree line of latitude, since it is the ring of latitude that divides the Earth exactly in half, between the North and South Pole. The Equator is where God's sign in the sky shines most directly on Earth most of the time. So, yes, obviously the Equator is one of the five major rings of latitude. The other four rings too are reminders of Earth's relationship with one of God's signs in the sky, the sun.

On the following diagram, you will find the ring of latitude called the **Arctic Circle** at nearly 66 degrees *north* of the Equator, the most northerly ring in the graphic. After you find it on this map, find the Antarctic Circle at nearly 66 degrees *south* of the Equator. These are two of Earth's important rings since they represent the most northern and southern locations where you could sit outside the whole day waiting for the sun to rise...and it never would. Yes, a day where the sun never rises but stays like the dark of *night* all *day* long!

142

You see, the further north or south that you go from Earth's important middle ring, the Equator, the more what season of the year it is effects how long the sun shines down upon you in a 24 hour period of time. Do you remember when we explored seasons and the solstices here on Earth? If you were sitting somewhere below the **Antarctic Circle** on June 21st, the June solstice, you could wait a whole 24 hours, and the sun would never appear. That is because the South Pole is facing away from the sun, while the North Pole is tilted towards the sun. On that same day of June 21st, you would be sitting for a whole 24 hours in sunlight if you were above the Arctic Circle.

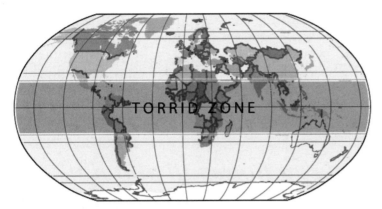

If you live between the ring of latitude called the Tropic of Cancer and the ring of latitude called the Tropic of Capricorn, you live in the Torrid Zone of balmy heat. If you live closer to the rings of latitude called the Arctic or Antarctic Circle, you live in more frigid temperatures—and likely own a snowsuit!

Then, six months later on December 21st, the December solstice, the land above the Arctic Circle sits in 24 hours of darkness while the land below the Antarctic Circle basks in 24 hours of sunlight.

You can see why these two rings of latitude, the Arctic Circle and the Antarctic Circle are important rings to Earth. These two rings remind her of where she is in her rotation around the sun—resulting in days without sunrise! Such an event is important indeed!

The remaining important 2 rings of latitude also are important to Earth during the solstices. Can you find the ring of latitude at 23 degrees north of the Equator? This is the most northerly location that you could see the sun directly overhead. At noon on June 21st, the sun is directly over this ring of latitude. With an important distinction like that, we refer to this ring of latitude as the **Tropic of Cancer**.

If you find the ring of latitude at nearly 23 degrees *south* of the equator, this is the most *southerly* location that sun may be seen directly overhead. On December 21st, at noon, you would see the sun directly overhead, if you were standing anywhere along this ring of latitude. This ring is called the **Tropic of Capricorn**. Might you guess what we call any of the area between the Tropic of Cancer and the

Standing in Namibia, on the south coast of Africa, we see a sign that marks the Tropic of Capricorn. Can you find Namibia on your globe?

Tropic of Capricorn—yes, the sunny, balmy tropics!

You have just learned all about Earth's 5 important rings: The Equator, the 2 Circles: the Arctic Circle and the Antarctic Circle, and the 2 Tropics: the Tropic of Capricorn and the Tropic of Cancer. While none of Earth's rings of latitude may be silver or gold like those of the jeweled lady I knew, they certainly are rings that flash and gleam in the brilliant sunlight, God's sign in the sky!

Well, world traveler, you've been to all of Earth's most important rings of latitude under the sun. You have also figured out how to discover how far *north* and *south* you are from the equator by determining your position of latitude! But it was *hundreds of years later* before geographers learned how to accurately determine from God's sky signs how far *east* or *west* they had traveled! What a stupendous feat THAT was! We'll save that tale for our next wild adventure that you'll certainly not want to miss!

Tell the folks at home all about it!

Can you put into your own words what you've just explored? (**Memory Joggers**: *What are Earth's five important rings of latitude? Can you explain why each is deemed important? The two circles? The two tropics? What do each of the important rings of latitude have to do with one of God's signs in the sky, the sun?*)

POSTCARD HOME

For now, why don't you grab a pen and write a postcard home, letting them know how travelers like you find your way around the world and not get lost! What can you share with someone what you have learned about latitude? What does parallel mean? What do you remember about the Greeks who worked on the grid? Can you explain to someone how you, as ship's captain, would find your position of latitude? Where is the starting point or 0 degree line of latitude? Where is the equator and what do you know about it? What does latitude measure? What are Earth's 5 important rings of latitude? You have so much to tell the folks at home!

(Postcard templates are available on the CD-ROM in the back of your book)

Reaching Out
to His World

This home of ours is a big place. With millions and millions of Moms and Dads, grandmas and grandpas, brothers and sisters all living in different rooms, or lands, of our Earth home. Do you know who may be living on our home of Earth at the same degree of latitude away from the sun as you are?

What can you do to reach out to the people living at the same degree of latitude from the equator as you live on?

- Grab a globe and find what parallel of latitude you live on. Then see what countries lie on the same ring as you do.

- Do some research online, at your library or through your bookshelves about one or two of those countries who live at the same degree of latitude north or south of the Equator as you do. Do they experience the same climate as you do? (Or does an ocean current dramatically change their climate?) What language do they speak? How does their country look the same or different than your country?

- Pray every day this week for families in one or two of those countries. Pray that they will feel God close to them this week, that they will know Him personally, and that they will be encouraged as they go about their daily tasks.

- Go online and see if you can find an email penpal from someone living on the same parallel of latitude as you do. Ask them about life where they live. Show them God's kind of love in your letters.

- Find a missionary (online or sponsored by your community of faith) who lives at the same degree of latitude as you do. Learn more about their needs, what it is like serving where they serve, and how they experience one of God's sky signs, the sun, and the weather it creates, where they live. Partner with them in the ministry by praying for them.

Learn about the people living on your line! Reach out with the love of God to your neighbors in our home of Earth!

Further Explorations

Maps and Globes *by Jack Knowlton*

(Gr. 1-5) Follow maps to the peak of the world's tallest mountain or to the dark depths of the ocean. Grab this book and head out to discover the world! This colorful book introduces the basics of maps and globes, latitude and longitude, scale and the differences between physical and political maps. Easy to understand, with simple, informative illustrations. Go for a spin around the world!

Where am I?: the story of maps and navigation *by A.G. Smith*

(Gr. 4-8) A captivating read that explores the history of cartography begins with the Yukaghir people and their birch-bark maps and follows mapmaking and navigation through Ptolemy, the ancient Chinese maps, the invention of the compass, the work of Mercator's, and the mapping of what is now North America.

Small worlds: maps and mapmaking *by Karen Romano Young*

(Gr. 3-7) Join the author and land at Chicago's O'Hare Airport. Use a map of the terminal (shown in full-page illustration) to help navigate through the tremendous building to arrive at the connecting gate. Then launch into a tour of many different types of maps with a variety of color drawings and photographs. Navigate through neighborhoods, cities, states, the globe, or even leave the planet and follow maps through outer space!

Mapping the world *by Sylvia A. Johnson*

(Gr. 4-6) Make your way through the history of cartography from an early Babylonian image scratched into a clay tablet to sophisticated modern maps developed with satellite and computer technology. Read more of early mapmakers and geographers: Ptolemy; Matthew Paris; Martin Waldseemller, the first cartographer to identify the New World as "America"; and Gerardus Mercator. Go traveling!

Too-Fun-to-Resist Excursion!

WHERE IN THE WORLD ARE YOU?

Did you know that wherever you are in the world, you can find your position of latitude—even if you don't have a sextant! You may never be a captain of a ship at sea, but all world travelers should know how to find their way around our home of Earth! All you need to find your position of latitude God gave you—your eyes and your hands!

Materials:
~ a good eye
~ a dark sky
~ two hands!

Ready To Go? Let's Head Out!

~ After the sun sets tonight, can you stare up at God's signs in the sky and find the **North Star**? To find the North Star, first, you have to find the **Big Dipper**. Found in the northern sky, the Big Dipper looks like a big cup with a long handle. Different times of the year, the Big Dipper will look different. In the late winter and early summer, the Big Dipper will be on its side or upside down. If you live far enough North, you will see the Dipper through summer and fall, when the cup is upright.

~ Once you have the Big Dipper, find the two stars that make the forward edge of the cup. If you draw a line from the bottom star, through the top star at the lip of the cup, follow that line for about 2 fist-lengths and you'll arrive at the North Star.

~ Now that you have found the North Star, you measure the angle that North Star makes with the Northern horizon below it. How does a geographer like you measure that angle? Well, if you have hands, you can measure it! Did you know that if you ball up your fist, the distance across your fist is about 10 degrees?

~ So, place your fist straight in front of you with the bottom of your fist resting on the horizon line. Now count how many fists you can stack up before your fist reaches the North Star or Polaris. Multiply the number of fists by 10 degrees—and THAT is your position of **LATITUDE**!!

~ Check with the real latitude of your town. How accurate were your measurements?

(If you are in the Southern Hemisphere: Look up in the night sky for God's sign of the **Southern Cross**. The Southern Cross is group of five stars that form a little cross. Facing South, two very bright stars in the Milky Way will be seen quite near the horizon, one roughly above the other. These are—from above down—**beta Centauri (Hadar)** and **alpha Centauri (Rigil Kentauri)**. These bright stars are typically called "**The Pointers**" as they point toward the Southern Cross. Drawing a line from alpha through beta, continue up a very short distance and you will discover the Cross lying on its left side—then use the same fist method to determine your position of latitude!)

(If you are finding it difficult to pinpoint any of these night stars, you can find maps of the night sky online. Just do a Google search of web images for the North Star or the Southern Cross and you'll soon be on your way!)

Too-Fun-to-Resist Excursion!

LIVING ON MY LINE!

The lines of latitude are, of course, imaginary lines, only drawn on maps. But folks all around the world live at the same degree of latitude as you do; they are "living on your line!" Can you find what other cities in the world are at the same degree of latitude as you?

Materials:
~ a globe or map marked with the lines of latitude
~ pencil and sheet of paper

Ready To Go? Let's Head Out!

~First, can you locate where in the world you are? What degree of latitude do you live at? Is that north or south of the Equator?

~ Draw a long line on your piece of paper. Sketch a picture of you or your home in the middle of your line. Jot down the name of your city under your little picture. Then, at the end of that line, write down the degrees of latitude you live at.

~ Mark one end of your line West and the other end of your line East.

~ Now, looking at your map, trace your line of latitude with your finger to the East. Write down the names of the cities that live "on the same line" as you do around the world. And what cities live to the West of you on the same line of latitude.

~ What does it mean to live on the same line of latitude? All the people who live in all of those cities, at the same degrees of latitude as you, are the same distance away from the equator as you are! They are just as far North or South from the equator as you are! All the way around this world! You are all living on the same line! And God knows each and every one of you by name!

GOD'S GREAT SIGNS AND IMAGINARY LINES

Chapter 11
(Part 2)

(Pack an ORANGE with you as we head out on this geographical adventure!)

Trek to the North Pole—up, up, up.
Tramp to the South Pole—down, down, down.
Can't find Poles West or East—looking around, around, around!

You would be on one very long expedition, indeed, if you set out in search of the East or West Pole! I suppose one could always be like Christopher Robin and Winnie the Pooh and just stick a wooden pole anywhere into the ground and *call* it the West Pole or the East Pole. But that really wouldn't be the East or West Pole, either, would it? There really isn't an East Pole or West Pole *anywhere* on Earth. (Maybe that is the reason why God says He has removed our sins as far as the East is from the West (Ps. 103:12)!) Because neither the East Pole nor West Pole exist as fixed points anywhere on Earth—well, you'll see what kind of mind-boggling riddle that created for world travelers!

On our last expedition, do you remember how geographers used THREE fixed points, the North Pole, the South Pole and the Equator, to determine a position of **latitude**? Let's sing that little diddly latitude song we hummed while we munched on our apple:

*"**Climbing the rungs of latitude, latitude, latitude.**
Climbing the rungs of latitude, north and south of the equator!"*

Climbing those rungs of latitude from the equator, up to the North Pole or down to the South Pole, explorers like us determine how far **north** and **south** we've journeyed by looking for an angle. Do you remember what angle we look for? Yes! We look for an angle from one of God's signs up, up, up in the sky, such as the North Star, then down, down, down to the horizon, where earth meets the sky. When we know that angle, we can determine how far *north* and *south* we've climbed those rungs of latitude!

But how do we discover how far *east* or *west* we have trekked around the world? We may know how far up, up, up north or down, down, down south we've journeyed, but how do we figure how far round east or west we've tramped around the globe of Earth?

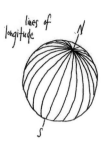

Now might be a fitting time to delve into our backpacks and pull out an orange. (World travelers always pack an ample food supply! Don't nibble just yet!) Peel the skin off your orange, and notice the lines of each section of the orange. The lines of each of those sections are much like the lines that geographers draw on maps known as "*meridians of longitude*." Drawing lines or meridians of longitudes that run from the North Pole down, down, down to the South Pole allow geographers to find their *east-west* position in the world!

Meridians are <u>not</u> parallel to other meridians of longitude, like parallels of latitude are. Meridians of longitude are imaginary lines that converge or meet at the North and South Poles. Meridians of longitude run from the North Pole to the South Pole and measure how far <u>east</u> or <u>west</u> you are of the Prime Meridian.

Longitude refers to an angle of distance telling you how far around *east* or how far around *west* you have traveled on our home we call Earth. These imaginary meridians of longitude that run from pole to pole along the surface of the Earth divide the globe into 360 equal slices—which would make for one VERY large orange, wouldn't it!?

Unlike the lines of latitude, the distances between the *meridians of longitude* are *not* parallel. Looking at your orange, do you notice that the widest part of each of your orange sections is right in the middle of the section? The distance between each of the meridians of longitude is also the widest at the middle section of Earth, the equator. At the equator, there are about 69 miles between each of the meridians of longitude. As you approach the poles, however, the distance between meridians decreases. The meridians of longitude actually meet or intersect at the North and South Pole, just like your orange sections meet at the top of the orange!

Let's sing another little song (again, to the tune of "*The Wheels on the Bus*"). Trace the lines of our orange sections as we sing along:

"It's a LONG, LONG way from pole to pole, pole to pole, pole to pole.
It's a LONG, LONG way from pole to pole, so we call these longitudes!"

Now every time you savor a juicy orange, think of the meridians of longitude running from pole to pole so explorers may know how far <u>east</u> or <u>west</u> they've traveled around the globe!

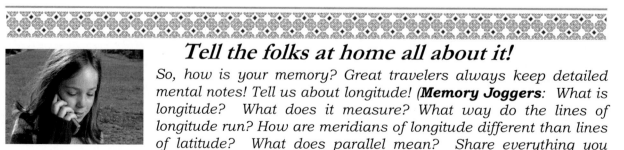

Tell the folks at home all about it!

*So, how is your memory? Great travelers always keep detailed mental notes! Tell us about longitude! (**Memory Joggers**: What is longitude? What does it measure? What way do the lines of longitude run? How are meridians of longitude different than lines of latitude? What does parallel mean? Share everything you remember about meridians of longitude. Can you sing our longitude song again? FABULOUS!) Let's keep humming along on our little exploration!*

Do you recall what the first line of latitude was? Yes! The equator! The equator was the fixed point that geographers used to divide the world in half. One half was NORTH of the equator while the other half was SOUTH. Once the equator was agreed upon as the first line of latitude, sailors everywhere could write letters home saying, "I am 40 degrees *North* or *South* of the Equator."

So if the first line of **latitude** is the **equator**, where would the first line of **longitude** be? With no fixed points of an East Pole or West Pole, and thus no middle fixed point in between, which meridian would be **THE FIRST** meridian of longitude to divide the world in half?

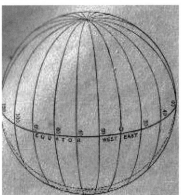

The Earth's imaginary line of the equator is a circle containing 360 degrees. You can divide the Earth's equator into 36 equal parts of ten degrees each. Then imagine drawing an even line between the North Pole through each of these division markings, and down to the South Pole. Each of the lines you drew through the poles would be at right angles to the equator and are called Meridians of Longitude!

Geographers refer to this first line of longitude as the **prime meridian**, since "**prime**" means *first* in Latin. Just like travelers needed a starting point of latitude, the equator, they also needed a starting point of longitude to say, "I am 50 degrees *East* or *West* of the prime meridian." But no one could agree on where to draw that prime meridian! EVERY country thought of their country as the center of the Earth. A wrestling match of sorts broke out between countries of the world for the honor of having the Prime Meridian run through THEIR country!

In Greenwich, England, you can stand on the Prime Meridian! Can you see the red painted line that marks the first line of longitude? Would you like to stand in the Eastern Hemisphere or in the Western Hemisphere?

Many folks considered Jerusalem, the city of King David, to be the center of the Earth. So they yanked for the Prime Meridian or first line of longitude to run through the Holy City. But the French pulled that Paris should have the prime meridian, while the Americans wrestled for Washington. This scrapping and scuffling went on for years and years. Until a town you probably have never even heard of, named Greenwich in England, finally won the whole contest. (You'd think Greenwich would rhyme with sandwich but it doesn't—you pronounce it Gren-itch—like a word with an itch!)

So Greenwich, England has the honor of having the first line of longitude run through it, dividing the world into half. On one side of the **Prime Meridian** lies the **Eastern hemisphere**, and on the other side lies the **Western hemisphere**. (You can actually go to the Royal Observatory in Greenwich and stand astride of the Prime Meridian—with one foot in the Eastern Hemisphere and one foot in the Western Hemisphere!)

Tell the folks at home all about it!

*Let's catch our breath again! What have you learned from your travels? (**Memory Joggers:** What is the first line of latitude? What is the first line of longitude called? Where did they decide to draw the imaginary line of the Prime Meridian? What does the Prime Meridian divide the world into?) FANTASTIC! Ready to explore on?*

The world now had a starting line of longitude, the Prime Meridian, looping from the North Pole, through Greenwich, England, and down to the South Pole. But how are you, as captain of a ship, riding the swelling high seas, going to find *your* position of longitude? How do you determine how far *east* or *west* you've traveled from the Prime Meridian at Greenwich, England? God wisely placed a sign in the sky so world travelers can know exactly how far east or west they have journeyed: the sun! The word "**meridian**" actually comes from the Latin word meaning "*noon,*" the time when the sun is directly overhead of a certain place.

If you still have your orange, slowly turn it completely around. That one entire spin around is called a "*turn of 360 degrees.*" Do you remember how long it takes for the Earth to completely spin around 360 degrees? Yes, the Earth spins an entire 360 degrees every 24 hours. That means in one hour of time, the Earth turns 1/24th of a complete turn. Or, to put it another way, the Earth turns 15 degrees every hour. After 24 hours, the Earth has fully turned right around 360 degrees.

Now, none of us ever get dizzy as the Earth turns its 360 degrees every day or 15 degrees every hour. The only way we even know we are turning is by looking up at God's big sign in the sky, the sun. When you wake up in the morning, the Earth is turned such that the sun is in the **east** of our sky and as the Earth turns, our position under the sun moves so that it appears like the sun is moving across

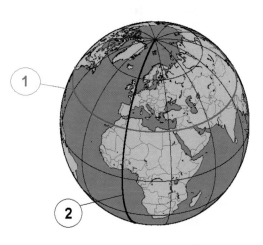

The black line marks the Prime Meridian, while the red line notes a ring of latitude. The intersecting co-ordinates of lines of longitude and parallels of latitude allow us to easily determine locations the globe over!

You do not notice us turning here on Earth, but God's sign in the sky, the sun, appears to move 15 degrees from east to west in the sky every hour—but it is actually the Earth that is turning!

Explorers hundreds of years ago sailed the seas with their eyes on God's signs in the sky—watching the North Star to determine latitude, and on the sun to determine time in locating their position of longitude.

NASA

the sky to the **west**. The sun is our sign in the sky, telling us that the Earth has turned another 15 degrees during every hour of time.

Since the sun appears to move 15 degrees in an hour, if you knew the sun's position in the sky overtop of the Prime Meridian running through Greenwich, England, and the sun's position in the sky, at the very same moment, over your location, you could figure out the difference in time. That difference in time could then be converted to a difference in position of longitude! But since only God can be in two places at the very same time, what would you need to tell you where the sun is in the sky in both of those places?

Yes, it is right there on your wrist—a watch! Who would have thought a clock would be necessary to finding our way around our Earth home! But a watch really is just an instrument that tells you the exact position of God's sign, the sun, up in the sky. When your wristwatch reads 11 a.m., it is simply informing you that God's sign, the sun, is getting high up in the middle of the sky.

As the ship's captain, a clock—actually 2 clocks—would be critical in determining your position of longitude out there on the endless sea of rolling blue. Every day while you tossed the ocean's waves, you would reset one of your clocks to noon. (Noon is the time when the sun reaches its very highest point overhead in the sky.) Then you would observe the time of the second clock. The second clock would be set to where the sun is in the sky over Greenwich, England. For example, let's say that second clock read 2 o'clock in the afternoon. The difference from the ship's time, 12 o'clock noon, and the time at Greenwich, 2 o'clock, is a difference of 2 hours. Remember that the sun appears to travel through 15 degrees of a turn every hour. We have traveled exactly 2 X 15 degrees, or 30 degrees, from the Prime Meridian at Greenwich.

Tell the folks at home all about it!

*Every traveler likes to tell tales. Why don't you tell us some of yours? (****Memory Joggers****: How many degrees does the world turn in 24 hours? How many degrees does the world turn in one hour? What has God put in the sky to help us determine how the world is turning? What could you use to tell you where the sun is in the sky in another place? Can you explain how you as sea captain could find your position of longitude?) MAGNIFICENT! Now, are you ready for more adventure on the high seas?!*

Finding your position of longitude seems relatively simple, doesn't it? Oh, but for years and years—HUNDREDS of years—it was nearly *impossible* for sea captains like you to find their position of longitude! Why, you ask?

Because they had clocks like I once had. With a big white face and stark black numbers, my clock lied. The clock's hands told me it was 9:00 am when it truth it was actually 9:15 am! My slow, lying clock may have made me late for church. But a lying clock out at sea might leave a sailor with a sinking ship!

If an hourglass causes a sailor to miscalculate the time by as little as even 2 seconds per hour, the sailor can find himself in a disastrous place longitudinally— and with a sinking boat crashed on rocks!

A lying clock, chiming the wrong time, is deadly business for a sea captain like you. For instance, imagine yourself setting out on a three-month voyage across the ocean. And, unbeknownst to you, one of your clocks, set to the time in Greenwich, slows down every hour by just a mere 2 seconds. After ninety days at sea, your lying clock would be running 72 minutes slower than the true time. Thus your longitude calculations would now be amiss by a full 18 degrees! When calculating the difference in time between your location at sea, and the time in Greenwich, you might believe you had sailed 60 degrees west of the Prime Meridian. But, truth be told, one of your clocks has lied to you by 2 seconds every hour, and you have actually sailed *78* degrees west! Now, instead of clear blue waters ahead of you, directly before you looms a wall of rocks! CRASH! Your lying clock fooled you into thinking you were safely sailing at 60 degrees west longitude—when you actually were much farther west, dangerously drifting into a rocky shore!

For hundreds of years there wasn't a single clock ANYWHERE in the whole wide world that could tell the truth at sea. All clocks lied, either speeding up or slowing down, as they rocked and tossed on the wild, waving ocean. With no clocks to keep accurate time, even the greatest of sea captains could easily misjudge his position of longitude. So, sadly, thousands of sailors drowned. Those who did arrive at their destination only got there by the grace of God!

Desperate to save sailor's lives, the King of England himself finally offered a reward to anyone who could solve the "**Problem of Longitude**." Whoever could develop a way to accurately determine longitude would win the prize of the King's ransom—more than $9 million dollars! Could anyone invent a clock that would not lose or gain more than three seconds in a day? Could any clock rock and roll for 40 days up and down across the frothy Atlantic Ocean, through storming, thunderous nights and searingly hot days—and still allow sailors to find their position of longitude within half a degree?

Scientists thought such a clock would never be invented. So they thought of other ideas: like anchoring ships every seven miles across the whole distance of the ocean. These ships would fire off cannons to announce to nearby ships the exact time. Can you imagine how many ships would be needed for such a task!? Obviously, the judges decided *that* was a bad idea: too much money for all those ships!

There were even crazier ideas. Ideas like a strange potion that would make a wounded dog, aboard a ship, howl every day when it was noon in Greenwich. The judges declared that idea VERY bad: who would want to make a poor dog stay wounded for a three month long ocean journey?

Finally, a carpenter's son, John Harrison, had an idea. When he was a youngster of six, lying ill in bed, John Harrison had been given a watch for amusement. For hours he had lain in bed listening to the tick of that clock. He had studied the tock of the clock's moving parts. When John Harrison became a man, he devoted his life to inventing a truth-telling clock that could keep time perfectly.

This 1767 portrait of John Harrison honors the ingenious man who solved the centuries old problem of determining longitude at sea.

Mr. John Harrison set to work to build such a clock. After five long years of toiling, he finally finished a 72-pound (32 kg) clock—which is probably heavier than you are! It only lost 10 seconds a day as it rocked away across the ocean. But John Harrison thought he could make a clock that would keep time even *better* time than that! Over twenty-seven long years of great thinking and diligence, John Harrison built 3 more clocks. Finally, in 1761, John Harrison produced what he called "THE watch." This masterpiece clock was just five inches across and weighed only 3.1 pounds (1.4 kg) (now that clock would weigh a lot LESS than you. John Harrison's final clock now only weighed as much as three blocks of butter.) When this clock rocked and rolled away at sea for over ninety long days, it had lost only a mere five SECONDS!

Unschooled but brilliant, John Harrison had solved the problem of finding the position of longitude! He had invented a clock that could be tossed and pitched upon the high seas all over the world, and still tell the unwavering truth. Those truth-telling clocks ensured that any sailor, anywhere, could now accurately pinpoint his position of longitude!

Tell the folks at home all about it!

*Whew! Aren't you relieved that the problem of longitude was solved! What a tale! I want to hear it all over again! Tell me, what caused the problem of longitude? (**Memory Joggers**: What happened if you were a traveler with a lying clock? How did a lying clock affect how you would calculate your position of longitude? Tell me as much as you can remember about how the solution was found! Do you remember any of the bad ideas that were not very good solutions?)*

Today we can hardly imagine that a man would devote his life to invent a clock that simply told the truth, or that an invention of a watch that kept true time, just like the watch on your wrist, could win a prize of 9 million dollars! Wasn't the whole wide world desperate for a way to know their position of longitude?

Now, 250 years later, our world is dramatically different from that long ago world which frantically labored to find a solution to the problem of longitude. Today, a geographer like you no longer needs 2 clocks to find your position of longitude. Nor do you now even need to know the time at the Prime Meridian in Greenwich. But time, and looking up, is still the key factor in knowing where you are!

Travelers now use GPS units when trekking out on an adventure. Isn't a GPS receiver very different than the tools travelers throughout history have used to determine where they are in the world?

Instead of a watch on the wrist, sailors and pilots, hikers and explorers now simply carry something called a GPS receiver in their pocket. "GPS" is the shortened, abbreviated way of saying "**global positioning system.**" "GPS," then, is a system that allows you to find your position on our globe.

This navigation global positioning satellite (GPS) sends signals to explorers and travelers on planes, boats, and on the ground so adventurers everywhere can determine their position of longitude and latitude.   *NASA*

Over ten thousand miles (16,090 km.) way up, up, up in space, far beyond the Earth's atmosphere, are 24 GPS satellites. These satellites circle all the way around our earth twice a day. Each of these satellites contains its very own clock. As these satellites circle our globe, each satellite sends a signal down to earth telling the satellite's own time and position. Travelers then carry a GPS receiver to receive these satellite signals of time and position. The GPS receiver compares the time a signal was sent out by a satellite with the time that signal was received on earth. That time difference tells the GPS receiver how far away the satellite is. With the distance measurements from at least two more satellites, the receiver can calculate for the travelers their exact position of longitude and latitude on our earth!

We now employ global positioning systems to determine our location, instead of clocks, yet regardless of where in the world you are, whether you are rocking quietly out on a boat on a starlit night, or standing on the peak of a snowcapped mountain as the sun rises; whether you are bumping along on the back of a camel across desert sand dunes or swinging with a troop of monkeys in a humid, lush jungle; no matter WHERE in the world you are, you can always look up, up to the heavens. And, there, looking down at you is Someone who always knows just EXACTLY where you are. For He, God Himself, made you, and this home, our Earth, and the signs in the sky. So, like travelers for thousands of years have done, keep one eye on your map and the other looking up, up, UP!

POSTCARD HOME

Good for you! You have traveled all around the globe, east to west, and made it back home! And the sites you have seen and the things you have discovered! Tell me about GPS— what does it mean? What does the receiver do? What do the satellites do? How many satellites are there and what does each contain? How does the receiver locate your position of longitude and latitude? How has GPS changed the way travelers find their location?

Can you whip out your pencil and a postcard? Why not draw a picture of your favorite part of today's geographical adventure? Then write a note on the back of your post card and make sure you tell the folks at home about the Prime Meridian and how you find your position of longitude. Remember to put your card on your ring with the rest of your postcard travels!

(Postcard templates are available on the CD-ROM in the back of your book)

Reaching Out
to His World

Hey, do you have the time? Sometimes we don't take the time to care for other people. Sometime we don't even know what time it is! Maybe today we can find the time!

Of course you remember that our Earth is round and that it takes Earth 24 hours to turn around on its axis. That means that if you stood in one spot, with the sun in the middle of the sky, you would have to stand there for a whole 24 hours before the Earth rotated around such that the sun would again be in the middle of the sky. If the sun were in the middle of your sky, what time would you set your watch to? Yes, 12 o'clock, lunchtime!

As the Earth rotates 15 degrees every hour, the sun is directly over different places at different times. Thus if everyone set their watch according to when the sun was over their heads, wherever they are, you might find your watch reading 12 noon, while the town clock of the village to your west reads 11:50 and your friend to your east is cleaning up lunch since its 12:10 pm. It would be pretty difficult to arrive anywhere on time, even if you did find your lost shoes just in time to leave several minutes early!   If each town set their own time according to when the sun was right in the middle of the sky over their town, nearly everyone everywhere would have a different time!

 A wise Canadian named Sir Sanford Fleming divided the Earth into 24 imaginary strips or zones, one for each hour of the day. Each zone is an hour ahead of the zone to the west of it. So 12 o'clock noon is set at the Prime Meridian in Greenwich, England. Then each time zone to the east of the Prime Meridian is one hour later, and every time zone to the west of the Prime Meridian is one hour earlier, until they meet at the International Date Line. The International Date Line runs along the 180th meridian of longitude, half way around the world from the Prime Meridian.   The International Date Line is the point at which geographers decided to have one day end and a new one begin. No matter what time of day it is, as soon as you have crossed the International Date Line, time changes one full day. If it is 7 a.m. Wednesday on one side of the International

Date Line, it is now 7 a.m. Thursday on the other side of the Date Line. If you fly west from Canada to Australia, you leap a day ahead the moment you cross the International Date Line. Then if you fly east from Australia, back home to Canada, you fall back a day. Just like a starting line on a racetrack divides one race lap from the next, so the International Date Line divides one day from the next.

What can you do to reach out to the people who live according to the same time as you do? You may be eating breakfast at your kitchen table looking at a flurry of snowflakes whirling white outside your window. At the same time, another child may be taking their bowl of cereal out to eat on the porch to better catch the ocean breezes and the warm morning sunshine. Both of your clocks on the wall read the exact same time---but your different positions of latitude means something dramatically different is happening outside your window!

- Find a world map of all 24 times zones on the CD-ROM in the back of the book—or visit http://wwp.greenwichmeantime.com/info/timezonemap.htm to view and print one out.

- Write down the names of countries that live on your time, in your time zone. According to their position of latitude, how might families in those countries experience life in our world differently than you do? Today, as you eat your meals, as you look at your watch, as you play and read and live in your home, think of what other children might be doing in those countries—looking at the exact same time on the wall as you are.

- Throughout your day, pray for people living on the same time as you are. Now that you have the right time, take the time to care!

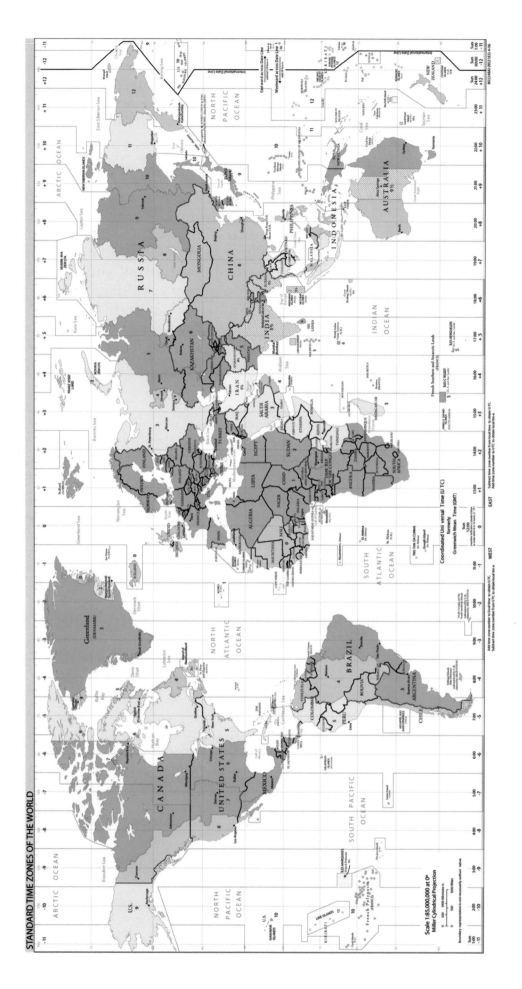

STANDARD TIME ZONES OF THE WORLD

160

Further Explorations

The Longitude Prize *by Joan Dash*

(Gr. 6–8) This is a fascinating story highlighting the life of John Harrison, the British clockmaker, who invented a brilliant method of measuring longitude out on the tossing waves.

The Illustrated Longitude *by Dava Sobel*

Don't miss this captivating read of how 18th-century scientist and clockmaker John Harrison solved one of the most challenging problems of all of history. This beautiful, colorfully illustrated edition gives readers a satisfying sense of the times, the players, and the intrigue of the longitudinal puzzle.

The Man Who Made Time Travel *by Kathryn Lasky*

(Gr. 4-6) It's 1707. Nearly 2000 sailors and four ships have been lost off England's coast. Parliament passed the Longitude Act guaranteeing 20,000 pounds sterling ($12 million today) for a method to navigate the seas with certitude. It was known that latitude could be measured, but to determine longitude-distance east or west of a point-a method had yet to be devised. In an engaging manner, Lasky relates the mad ideas that were considered, including barking dogs, tiptoeing, and a fire on deck before examining the inventive life and mind of a genius who solved the problem.

Latitude and longitude *by Rebecca Aberg*

All it takes are a few coordinates to locate Bear Cave, the international Date Line, and the equator in this lively introduction to the lines that run up and down and across on a map or a globe—latitude and longitude.

Sea Clock: The Story of Longitude *by Louise Borden*

(Gr. 3-5) This handsome, well-researched picture book introduces John Harrison, the 18th-century English carpenter turned clockmaker who spent more than 40 years perfecting a device that solved the centuries-old problem of determining longitude.

Latitude & Longitude *by Brian Williams*

This book is a discussion of the history of mapmaking and its relationship to navigation and the measurement of time.

Around the World in 80 Days *by Jules Verne*

(Gr. 6–up) On a wager with his chums at the Reform Club, Phileas Fogg attempts the trip described in the title of this classic adventure novel. Learn about time zones, international travel and more.

161

Too-Fun-to-Resist Excursion!

FIND ME!

It's been quite a trip around the world, exploring these parallels of latitude and meridians of longitude! Now, let's pull out our atlases and have some fun! Let's play hide and seek in our atlases! Think they can find you?

Materials

~ atlas
~ fun and imagination

Ready To Go? Let's Head Out!

Let's begin with a wee mind twister:

~ Can you find where you would be on Earth's surface when you are nowhere (neither north or south, east or west) Check for the answer at the end of this activity!)

~ Now, gather round the atlas with your fellow geographers. Each of you decide on three places you would like to visit. Look on your atlas or globe to find the location.

~ For each location, say one sentence that includes the cardinal directions (N-E-W-S), and "latitude" and "longitude."

How far east or west are you from the Prime Meridian (longitude) and how far north or south are you from the equator (latitude).

~ Can your fellow geographers find where in the world you are?

Enjoy finding each other on the pages of your atlas! What world travelers you are!

("Nowhere" is at the intersection of the Prime Meridian and the equator.)

Too-Fun-to-Resist Excursion!

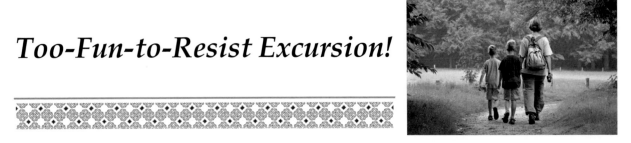

ZONED IN!

While you sit here reading this book, some children are brushing their teeth for bed, some children are brushing their teeth before breakfast, and some children simply aren't brushing their teeth at all (they are probably reading a book like you are!). All around our globe, people are getting up out of bed, going to bed, setting off to work, driving home from work—every one is living in their own zone. Time zone, that is. Would you like to know what zone the world is living in, right now?

Let's make a clock that tells the world's time zones!

Materials
~ scissors   ~ a brad
~ 2 paper plates
~ ruler and pen

Ready To Go? Let's Head Out!

~ Take one of your paper plates and cut the edge or rim completely off, leaving you with a flat circle.

~ Now, taking your ruler and pen, divide this paper plate into quarters. Now divide each of these quarters in half. Then divide each of these into thirds. You should have 24 equal, pie-shaped, sections.

~ Pick one section, and neatly write "London, Greenwich Time." Then, moving the same way as the hands of your clock does (clockwise), write "Paris." Continue, one section at a time, to write each of the names of the following cities:

Jerusalem	Brisbane	Mexico City
Moscow	Magadan	Washington
Abu Dhabi	Wellington	Caracas
Islamabad	Samoa	Buenos Aires
Dhaka	Honolulu	Atlantic Ocean
Jakarta	Anchorage	Greenland
Bejing	Vancouver	
Tokyo	Denver	

~ Now take your plate with all the city names and lay it on top of the other paper plate. Fasten the two plates together with a brad through the very center.

~ On the rim of your larger plate, right above the pie piece that reads "London," write your pen "12:00 midnight" Next to Paris, write 1:00 am. Above Jerusalem, write 2:00 am and so on, above each pie piece. When you come to write your next 12:00, be sure to write "noon" beside it (you should be at the Wellington pie piece). Continue writing the times, 1:00 pm. 2:00 pm until you arrive back at the London pie piece and 12:00 midnight.

~ Can you find the city that lives in your zone? What time is it in your time zone when it is midnight in London, England?

~ Now rotate the pie pieces around so the current time right now on your clock is above the name of the city in your time zone. Now you can "see" the time right now on the clocks of all those cities!

~ Looking at your world clock, can you picture in your mind where the sun is in the sky over those cities? Who is brushing their teeth on their way to bed? Who is brushing their teeth just before breakfast? And who do you think is just like you - reading a book?

There is an appointed time for everything.
And there is a time for every event under heaven.
Ecclesiastes 3:1

Bags are Packed...Again!

At the end of every road is the beginning of another road. And so it is with this road.

We have finished the grand tour of the home God built for us, Earth. We've explored Earth's floor, the lithosphere. We've investigated Earth's water, the hydrosphere. And we've soared to Earth's heights, through the atmosphere. We've learned how to get around in our Earthly home—what with our maps, God's sky signs helping us determine a location's latitude and longitude, and our sense of direction, we can now determine where in the world we are!

At the end of this road we turn and look back at the wonders we have traversed: scraping fault lines and thunderous volcanoes, pulsing ocean currents and shimmering auroras, glowing fireball of the sun and back through all seven diverse continents! Each step along our way, we have been awed at our God who "**stretches out the north over empty space and hangs the earth on nothing**" (Job 26:7). We have marveled at Him who "**establishes the mountains by His strength, being girded with might**" (Ps. 65:6). Only our God alone could have "**gathered the wind in His fists... wrapped the waters in His garment [and] established all the ends of the earth**" (Prov. 30:4).

This is **His** glorious globe.

Separate images of the Earth and the moon, photographed from the spacecraft Galileo, captures the magnificence of this world God has created as a home for us all. *NASA*

He "made the heavens, the heaven of heavens with all their host, the earth, and all that is on it, the seas and all that is in them. [He] gives life to all of them_and the heavenly host bows down." (Neh. 9:6)

And so do we. We worship Him.

We see that though this part of the journey around His world has come to an end, that another journey is just about to begin. Another road lies before us, full of possibilities, a journey traipsing around His earth, meeting His people, sharing their lives, glorying in this home that He, our Creator God, has made for us all.

May I save you a seat right next to me when we head out again—for the countries around His glorious globe!

"You are the God who works wonders... among the peoples"

(Ps. 77:14)

166

Photo credits:

All repeating graphics throughout the text (for chapter headings, narration prompts, notebooking assignments, reading lists, and reaching out activities) are licensed through iStockPhotos by Knowledge Quest, Inc..

Diagrams (unless otherwise stated): A. Voskamp

All other photos are credited as stated in text or are from Wikimedia Commons and in the public domain.

USGS: United States Geological Survey
NASA: National Aeronautics and Space Administration
NOAA: National Oceanic and Atmospheric Administration

Cover Design: Jeremy Conn of Conn Creative Media

All Biblical quotations are from the New American Standard Bible.

QUICK ORDER FORM

Would you like your own copy? Or perhaps the sequel in this series entitled A Child's Geography: Explore the Holy Land. Simply indicate the products that interest you and get in touch with us in one of the ways below.

☐ A Child's Geography: Explore His Earth - $32.95

☐ A Child's Geography: Explore the Holy Land - $32.95

☐ Or request a free catalog and sampler CD which contains samples and entire ebooks which represent our line of quality history and geography resources meant to educate and entertain your students.

Fax Orders: Fax this form to (210)568-9655
Telephone Orders: Call 1(877)697-8611 with your credit card in hand
Mail Orders: Send this form to:

> **Knowledge Quest, Inc.**
> P.O. Box 789
> Boring, OR 97009
> (210)745-0203

Name:_____

Address:_____

City:_____State:_____Zip:_____

Telephone:_____

Email:_____

Subtotal for books indicated above:

US Shipping, please add $5 for single title and $2 for additional title:

Total amount enclosed:

Payment:

☐ check

☐ credit card (indicate type)

Card number:_____

Name on card:_____Expiration date:_____

Yes, we do sell wholesale as well. Need to contact us? Send an email to orders@knowledgequestmaps.com or visit us online at www.knowledgequestmaps.com